WALKING
IN MALLORCA

Walking in Mallorca

by

June Parker

CICERONE PRESS
Milnthorpe, Cumbria, England

Frontispiece: Pêna Roca path (Walk 2)

© June Parker
ISBN 0902 363 80 8
First published 1986
Reprinted 1988

Acknowledgements

The author would like to thank all the friends who gave advice and encouragement during the preparation of this book. Special thanks go to Alan Parker who came on all the walks and helped all the way from the first draft to finished product. The generosity of Tom Price, Ron Lyon, and Chris Lyon, who gave up their valuable time to reading the manuscript and made helpful suggestions is also much appreciated.

Front cover: The Cavall Bernat Ridge (Walk 8)
Back cover: Roca Blanca from Fumat (Walk 4)

CONTENTS

ROUTES

Graded list of walks

INTRODUCTION

General background

Mallorca is the largest of the Balearic islands and better known as a paradise for sun-worshippers than for walkers. That it is such a paradise is slowly being discovered by discerning walkers who enjoy the attractive and varied scenery, the equable climate and the opportunity to walk in places where other people rarely go. Add to this the extensive Mediterranean flora, the spring migration of birds and the opportunities for photography and it is hard to understand why it has been neglected as a walking area for so long. One reason is the inadequacy of the maps, another is the almost total lack of signposts, but the main reason is that until now there has been no guidebook in English written specifically for the experienced mountain walker.

The Balearic islands lie in the Mediterranean between Barcelona on the coast of mainland Spain and Algiers on the North African coast. This favoured position is responsible for the sunny, temperate climate attractive to both sun-lovers and walkers alike. Here it should be pointed out that the temperatures in July and August which are ideal for sunbathing are far too hot for any serious walking by the average person. These months are best avoided and the recommended 'season' for walkers is from the beginning of September to the end of May.

The main mountain chain in Mallorca is the Sierra de Tramuntana which lies along the north-west coast and reaches heights of over 1000m in many places, culminating in the Puig Mayor at 1450m. The Sierra de Levante in the east, although only topping the 500m contour also offers walks of surprising length and quality, having the same sort of high mountain characteristics as the Tramuntana. Many of the mountain tops of the island are almost bare of vegetation and the hard rough limestone gives excellent walking and scrambling with loose rock being extremely rare. There is a varied flora including dense evergreen forests, maquis and garigue in the arid zones and sub-alpine flora on the approach to the peaks.

The small size of the island means that almost every walk is enhanced by views of the coastline and the sea. The sea varies in colour from the palest greens and blues to incredible dark ultramarine and purple, often with small bays of white sand between steep cliffs which plunge dramatically into the water. In fact the coastal walks vie in attraction with the inland mountains and although they may not reach any great height often go through very wild and uninhabited

On the Cavall Bernat Ridge (Walk 8)

country.

Many of the walks in this guidebook go through pathless and rough areas where some experience of route-finding is needed. Some make use of excellent tracks and paths which are very easy to follow, while others use old paths which are neglected and overgrown and are almost impossible to find. There are a surprising number of good paths, but many of these are not shown on the maps (although some non-existent paths may be shown on the same map). Even when paths are mapped, they are rarely signposted, except the excellent paths recently developed by the conservation organisation ICONA. If using the maps to plan independent walks, care is required. Steep cliffs or very complex ground may be encountered in places where the map gives no indication of this.

Scope of this guide

This book is written for the experienced mountain walker who is used to walking in the British hills in all seasons. It is not comprehensive but provides a selection of walks of varying length and difficulty and should enable those limited to a short holiday to make the best use of their time. All the walks except one return to the starting point by a circular route whenever this is possible. Most depend on the use of a hired car, by far the best means of getting around on the island, but a few may be done directly from Cala San Vicente or Puerto Pollensa. When public transport can be used this has been pointed out, but in general the buses are geared to taking people to the beaches in summer and not walkers to the mountains in winter.

Accommodation and travel

Although development of the tourist industry in recent years has led to the spread of large concrete jungles, these are in the main confined to the coast around the bay of Palma from Paguerra to El Arenal. However, there is no need to stay in this area, there being plenty of accommodation throughout the island in places that remain reasonably unspoilt. In particular three resorts which make good centres for walking will be described in detail at the end of this section. If accommodation cannot be obtained in one of these resorts, due to last minute booking perhaps, then the next best thing is to be in or near Palma, from where escape to the hills can be made each day by the excellent network of roads radiating from the city. It is then possible to use either a hired car or public transport, get in a good walk and be back in time for the evening meal, as a Palma-based walking club does every Sunday all the year round.

One advantage of the tourist development of the island is the number of tour operators offering package holidays throughout the year, with the effect of keeping prices down to a very reasonable level. However much the idea of this is disliked, it is by far the cheapest way of getting there and need have no disadvantages if a careful choice is made. By shopping around it is possible to find a special offer which includes the use of a car either free or at a much reduced rate. These offers usually apply to the winter months but that is all to the good as winter is the best time for a walking holiday.

It is of course also possible to book a flight independently and find your own accommodation either in a hotel or an apartment. Apartments are often available over or adjoining small bars and bar-restaurants where meals may be had if desired. This sort of holiday is easier to arrange on a second visit when you know your way around, and also if you are able to speak Spanish a little. English is usually spoken in the larger hotels, but not always in the smaller places where you are most likely to find the cheaper accommodation. If you are going it alone, remember that some hotels do not open in winter, although those that do are rarely full. The exception to this is Christmas and New Year, and also Easter, when booking ahead is advisable.

If you are able to take advantage of a long stay winter holiday then extremely good rates can be obtained by staying for one month, two months or three months. If you are fortunate enough to have this amount of time then another option is to book a one-week package holiday at the beginning and another one-week at the end. This way gives time to look round and negotiate for an apartment on the spot plus two weeks in a hotel for about the same price as an independent flight would cost, plus free transport to and from the airport.

It is quite feasible to take your own car to Mallorca by using the cross-channel ferry, driving to Barcelona and taking another ferry from there to Palma. This is not advisable unless your time and financial resources are very extensive as the cost of the ferries, the overnight stops and the petrol make such a project very expensive.

There is one official camp-site on Mallorca, near Ca'n Picafort on the north east coast. If you wish to camp or bivvy in the mountains then permission should be asked at the nearest farm. In many areas there is a prohibition against lighting fires because of the risk to the dry vegetation. All walks can be done easily from a base in a small

11

town or village, but longer two or three-day walks carrying a small tent and food supplies could be worked out.

Choice of base

The three best resorts for walkers are Cala San Vicente, Puerto Pollensa and Soller. Cala San Vicente is a small quiet resort with sandy beaches and a spectacular view of the steep cliffs of the Cavall Bernat ridge across the sparking blue-green sea. Several walks start from here and it is no great distance to drive to the start of any of the other walks. There is a bus service too, although it is very limited and walkers need to catch the 08.45 bus to Pollensa during the winter.

There are several hotels here used by various tour operators and a number of apartments. Self-catering is no problem, with two or more supermarkets open all the year and easy access to the market in Pollensa on Sundays by the 10.00 bus.

Puerto Pollensa lies on the coast in a very sheltered position with some quiet hotels separated from the sea by a narrow strip of sand. Much development has taken place in recent years and is still going on, to its detriment perhaps, but it does have an attractive marina and more shops and buses than Cala San Vicente. There are more people about too, but it can be very calm and quite warm here on days when there is a blustery wind and a rough sea at Cala. It could be a better choice if you have children or non-walkers in your party.

Soller lies on the west coast between the mountains and the sea and is an excellent centre for walks, although there are some disadvantages. Because of its situation it has no protection from any westerly gales, and in the exceptional snow-falls of 1985 it was cut off for days at a time from the rest of the island. If you want to explore the rest of the island then you have to drive over the Coll de Soller (496m) at the beginning and end of the day, or drive along the winding corniche roads to the north and south. There are some hotels in Soller and many more in Puerto Soller, which is linked to the town by a fairly frequent tram service (See p.133). Not many tour operators offer holidays here, but it could be a good choice for the independent traveller who wants to concentrate on the walks in this area.

In summer it is possible to make use of the bus which runs daily from Soller to Puerto Pollensa in order to do some of the walks in this guidebook, e.g. Massanella, the Canaleta de Massanella, the Morro d'Almallutx or the Torrente de Pareis. For this latter walk you would need to be sure of catching the bus back from Sa Calobra at 17.00, but this is a summer service only and one you would have to check on. This bus only runs on weekends in winter. (See p.124)

Deià is another possible base for walkers travelling independently. It is a small and very pretty village between Soller and Valldemossa, well-known as the chosen home of Robert Graves. Set on steep ground overlooking the sea and backed by high mountains, it attracts many painters, but also has the reputation of attracting poor weather in winter. There are a few small hotels, either in the village or in Lluch-Alcari a little further north, and rooms are available fairly cheaply. There is a bus service linking Deià with Soller and Puerto Soller to the north and Valldemossa and Palma to the south, but it is not very frequent and in the winter the early morning bus in both directions does not run. (See p.123)

Climate and weather

The climate of Mallorca is a typical Mediterranean one: that is the winters are mild, the summers are hot and dry and there is plenty of sunshine all the year round. The relative humidity is very constant throughout the year at about 70%. This, together with the sea breezes, makes even the hottest summer days pleasant and enjoyable, provided you are not trying to walk on the mountains. There are almost 300 sunny days during the year and even in the winter months there is an average of five hours of sunshine each day.

When rain falls it often does so in sharp heavy showers that soon clear up, except for occasional days of torrential rain which can occur in the late autumn and early spring. There can, of course, be different weather conditions in different parts of the island. Naturally the rainfall is greatest over the highest mountains, varying from 1000mm per year near the Puig Mayor to less than 400mm on the south coast. It is thus often possible to find a sunny or sheltered place to walk by avoiding the highest peaks on bad days.

Snow is quite common on the mountain tops. So common that it was formerly collected during the winter months to make ice for use in the summer. (See p.31) At sea level it is very rare and there was great excitement when several inches fell in January 1985. Local people said it was the first time it had happened for 29 years. Although only inches fell at the coast, it was several feet deep in the mountains. (See photograph taken on the Puig de Maria, page 69)

The central plain, protected by the high Sierras to the north west enjoys an almost sub-tropical climate. In winter the average mid-day temperature here is 10°C, whereas it is 6°C on the north west coast.

Temperatures in °C and no. of rainy and sunny days each month

	Jan.	Feb.	Mar.	April	May	June	July	Aug.	Sep.	Oct.	Nov.	Dec.
Max.temp.*	14	15	17	19	22	26	29	29	27	23	18	15
Min.temp.*	6	6	8	10	13	17	19	20	18	14	10	8
Average	9	8	11	13	17	21	26	24	22	18	14	12
Sea temp.	13	13	15	16	18	21	24	26	22	19	17	15
Rainy days	8	6	6	7	4	2	2	1	5	8	8	9
Sunny days	23	22	25	23	27	28	29	30	25	23	22	22

* Min.temp. at dawn, max, temp. at midday.

QUERCUS COCCITERA (KERMES OAK)

GEOLOGY AND SCENERY

Brief geological history

The Balearic islands lie on a submarine sill extending north eastwards from Cape Nao on mainland Spain and are an extension of a chain of mountains in that area know as the Baetic Cordillera. These mountains are part of the Western Mediterranean block, pushed up in a major mountain-building episode at the end of the Carboniferous period, the Hercynian orogeny. It is thought that a ripple fold in a northeast/southwest direction was then thrown up by pressure from the northern land mass and that this fold now underlies the main mountain chain of Mallorca, the Sierra de Tramuntana.

Subsequent earth movements raised and lowered this block a number of times, with various land bridges uniting it temporarily with Europe and Africa. It is these land bridges that partly account for the variety of flora and fauna on the islands.

Major events in the Mezozoic period were the laying down of thick deposits of Triassic clays and marls, followed by Jurassic and Cretaceous limestones, when all southern Europe, the Mediterranean and North Africa was a synclinal basin under the sea known to geologists as the 'Tethys Sea'. Even during these times there were periods of uplift when the high land in the north was above water. During the Cretaceous there was probably a land-bridge with Catalonia.

In the following Eocene period massive earth movements caused folding of vast areas of southern Europe and North Africa. It was at this time that both Alpine and Himalayan folding and uplift occured. In Mallorca the pressure against the Hercynian block was responsible for further folding on the same axis as the original ripple fold. This and later folding and faulting along the same axis gave rise to steep scarp slopes facing north west with gentler slopes on the south east side.

A series of lakes was formed at the foot of these slopes when surface water was trapped above impermeable Jurassic rocks. Alluvial deposits dated at 50 million years, or late Eocene, are evidence of this.

A mainland bridge is believed to have existed in the lower Oligocene, then in the Miocene there was a further submergence with deep sea deposits being laid down over a wide area. At the end of the Miocene further elevation brought the mountain chain up again to its present height. The history after this is uncertain, except that the

Mallorca: simplified geological history

ERA	PERIOD	EPOCH	EVENTS	MYA
CAINOZOIC	QUATERNARY	Recent Pleistocene	Mallorca sep. from Menorca Ibiza sep. from Formentera	2
CAINOZOIC	TERTIARY	Pliocene	Bridge between Ibiza and Mallorca broken.	7
CAINOZOIC	TERTIARY	Miocene	Elevation & uplift to present height. More deep sea deposits	19
CAINOZOIC	TERTIARY	Oligocene	Partial re-submergence, but with land bridges	38
CAINOZOIC	TERTIARY	Eocene Paleocene	Major folding & earth movements	63
MESOZOIC	CRETACEOUS	Upper Lower	Land bridge to Catalonia Deep sea limestones deposited	136
MESOZOIC	JURASSIC		Deep sea limestones deposited	190
MESOZOIC	TRIASSIC		Thick deposits of clays and marls laid down	225
PALAEOZOIC	PERMIAN		Ripple fold in N.E./S.W. direction	280
PALAEOZOIC	CARBONIFEROUS		Hercynian mountains formed	345
PALAEOZOIC	DEVONIAN		Fossil plants show earliest evidence of life	410
PALAEOZOIC	SILURIAN ORDOVICIAN CAMBRIAN		? ? ?	

MYA = Million Years Ago

islands did not achieve their present form until late in the Quaternary.

Surface features today

Although most of the exposed rocks on Mallorca are limestones of various ages and the Triassic clays and marls, mention must be made of other rocks that will be observed from time to time during the walks. There are a fair number of minor igneous intrusions of a dark doleritic rock, probably of Triassic age, seen for example in the Ternelles valley. In the north east of the island there are some extensive areas of very coarse conglomerates in which rounded pebbles and boulders with all sorts of angular fragments are well cemented together, giving a 'pudding-stone' appearance. This can be seen easily on the walk to the Puig de S'Aguila (Walk 10). Here too there is an outcrop of an attractive pink, white and black rock, not a true marble, but the result of pressure and percolating solutions acting on the limestone. Occasional outcrops of cross-bedded sandstones are also seen, as in the village of Cala San Vicente for example.

There are three distinct areas of Mallorca which can be considered as structural-morphological units: these are the main mountain chain known as the Sierra de Tramuntana, the central plains and the mountains of the south-east, the Sierras de Levante.

1. The Sierra de Tramuntana

The Tramuntana is a chain of mountains some eighty km long which lies in a northeast/southwest direction along the line of the original ripple fold. There are twelve peaks and over thirty five tops more than 1000m in height. There are many ridges showing the same directional trend as the whole chain. The Cavall Bernat ridge (Walk 8) is one of these. The steep northwest scarp slopes are a striking feature, particularly the coastal scarp which makes much of the shoreline inaccessible. This feature is seen on the circuit of the Puig Roig (Walk 20) and on the approach to the Puig Gros de Ternelles (Walk 15). As pointed out elsewhere, these scarps are not always marked on the maps and this should be borne in mind when planning your own walks.

Many of the rocks at the surface are deep sea calcareous rocks dating from the Miocene. They are hard medium-grey rocks often weathered into fantastic pinnacles and with conspicuous 'flutings' due to rainwater erosion. There are many extensive areas of typical 'karst' or limestone pavement, where percolating ground water has enlarged the joints into deep fissures called grikes. The ridges between, known as clints, can be knife sharp, and negotiating this sort of terrain calls for great care from walkers.

There is only one major watercourse on the island. This is the Torrente de Pareis (Walk 21), and it has worn through great thicknesses of rock to expose earlier Jurassic strata of a very dense hard limestone, sometimes dolomitic.

2. The central plains

The central plain or *es pla* consists of Miocene and late Plio-Pleistocene deposits. Large areas are completely flat and covered with a layer of *terra rossa*, a red and very fertile soil consisting of the insoluble residue left behind after the solution of limestone by ground water. The red colour is due to the accumulation of iron oxides.

Elsewhere there is an undulating relief, and at the south-eastern border of the Tramuntana is a belt of low hills derived by erosion from

17

the Sierras themselves. Occasional inliers of Triassic and Jurassic rocks rise up prominently from the central plain, such as Randa (548m).

3. *The eastern hills*

The Sierras de Levante are a lower range of hills running from the Artá peninsula towards Manacor and Felanitx. They only just exceed 500m in height. The folding here is considered to be more recent than that of the Tramuntana. Triassic and Jurassic strata are overlain by Cretaceous limestones and by the mid-grey Miocene limestone. There are extensive areas of karst and some large Jurassic cave systems near the coast. These are the caves of Drach, Hams and Artá and they are all open as show-caves.

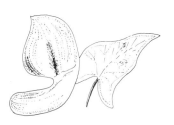

ARUM PICTUM

NATURAL HISTORY

The pleasure of walking on Mallorca is greatly enhanced by the rich variety of plant and animal life. Wherever you go you cannot fail to notice the immense variety of flowers and shrubs and how different the vegetation is from that seen in Britain. Ornithologists have been visiting the island for many years, mainly in the spring to catch the migrants, but there is plenty to interest the walker with a casual interest in bird-watching all the year round. The notes which follow are necessarily very brief and the reader is referred to the bibliography in the appendices for further reading.

Flora

There are not many varieties of native trees in the woodlands of Mallorca; only pine, oak, olive, carob and dwarf fan palm: other varieties, such as black poplar, London plane, ash, elm, hawthorn and blackthorn will be observed on the banks of streams. A striking feature of the Mallorcan forests and woodlands is how green they are in winter, not only because of the preponderance of evergreens but because the autumn rains wash off all the summer dust which gives a drab grey appearance to the trees. Both the pines and the oaks are perfectly adapted to the long hot and dry summers: the pines having leaves reduced to narrow grooved cylinders and the oaks having thick leathery leaves with a waxy coating, so that both types of tree cut down loss of moisture by transpiration.

The Aleppo pine *(Pinus halepensis)* grows from sea level up to 1000m and is abundant everywhere. It can be 20m high with a straight trunk but is frequently bent and twisted in windy situations. It often grows in fairly open stands but is sometimes in mixed woodlands with the evergreen oaks. Two other pines are seen but are not common; the stone pine or umbrella pine *(Pinus pinea)* recognisable by its 'umbrella' shape, and *Pinus halepensis var. ceciliae* which has upward growing branches.

Of the five different evergreen oaks the most common is the holm oak, *(quercus ilex)*. It has been much used in the past for the making of charcoal (See p.30) but is still abundant. Other varieties are the kermes oak, cork oak, Lusitanian oak, and *(Quercus rotundifolia)*. Bonner, (See Bibliography p.141), gives full details of how to recognise them and where to see them all.

It is not known whether the olive *(Olea europea)* existed wild on the island before it was domesticated. The sub-species, *(oleaster)*, does

19

exist, and it is believed that the cultivated olive was developed from this in Syria. Another sub-species, *(var. sylvestris)* also grows on the island.

The cultivated olive grows up to 10m in height and has a distinctive silvery-grey foliage. Olive groves are seen everywhere, on the plains and on terraces levelled out of the mountain slopes, where they will be noticed on many of the walks. Some of the trees are very old, possibly 1000 years or so and their gnarled and twisted trunks are very striking.

The carob tree is also very common. It is a beautiful tree with thick and shiny leaves. The new growth is a lighter green than the old, so that the tree often has a two-toned appearance. The fruits are conspicuous, being large pods which are green at first but become brown on ripening and eventually almost black. They have a high sugar content and are used to feed cattle.

The dwarf fan palm *(Chamaerops humilis)* is most distinctive with its sharp lance-like leaves arranged in fans. It occurs in three separate areas on Mallorca: the north-east near Cala San Vicente, Formentor and Alcudia, the Artá peninsula, and in the south-west near Andraitx.

Although trees are few in variety, there is such a wealth of flowering shrubs that it is quite impossible even to list them all here. Of the more outstanding ones which are to be seen on the walks in this book, the most common is the lentisk or mastic tree *(Pistacia lentiscus)*, a dark spreading evergreen shrub which grows from 1-3m high and has a resinous smell. This grows in all situations from sea level to high in the mountains. It is said that keeping a sprig between your lips wards off thirst however hot the day. The leaves have 3-6 pairs of dark green leaflets with blunt tips. The flowers occur in the leaf axils and are either reddish or brown, followed by fruits which are first red then black.

Very noticeable too are the beautiful blue flowers of the common rosemary *(Rosemarinus officinalis)*, a dense aromatic shrub with seems to bloom somewhere all the year round. The deepest blue flowers are seen on Formentor and on the Serra de San Vicens where in early April swarms of bees hum around each plant.

In March and April the yellow brooms burst into flower. First to be seen is *Genista lucida* in March, localised in the Artá area and the southwest, then the thorny broom *(Calicotome spinosa)* in April, easily recognised by its trifoliate leaves.

Hypericum balearicum, an endemic St. John's wort is another common shrub found on mountain slopes, in woodlands and by the roadside. The yellow flowers may be seen sporadically all the year round but it is at its best in the spring. The leaves are deep green, narrow and rather crinkled. There is another endemic St. John's wort, *Hypericum cambessedessii* which grows in the beds of mountain streams. It has the same flowers as *balearicum* but the leaves are long and flat and of a beautiful pale green which is almost luminescent.

Asphodels are everywhere, growing along roadsides and on barren wasteland from the seaside to the mountain tops. The tall spikes of white flowers with a reddish-brown vein on each petal are very conspicuous. In spite of its name, *Asphodelus microcarpus*, it may grow as much as 2m high. The plant does not seem to be eaten by animals and its presence is often a sign of neglected and overgrazed ground. There is a smaller variety *Asphodelus fistulosis*, which is less common. The flowers may be pink, but it is most easily identified by the leaves which are rounded in cross-section, those of *microcarpus* being V-shaped.

One of the most attractive groups of shrubs are the rock-roses which are commonly found in the oak woods as well as in more open spaces. Most common is *Cistus albidus*, or grey-leaved cistus which has velvety leaves and large pink crumpled flowers. It flowers in April-June and is very aromatic. *Cistus monspeliensis* or narrow-leaved cistus with smaller white flowers is also common and starts to flower in March. Slightly less common is the sage-leaved cistus, *Cistus salvifolius* with a large white flower.

The strawberry tree *(Arbutus unedo)* is a very striking tree-like shrub with big shiny leaves and fruits which turn first orange then deep red in October and November. The fruits, which are edible but tasteless, ripen at the same time as the white flowers of the following year's crop are in bloom.

Tree heather *(Erica arborea)* grows up to 3m high and is dense but feathery looking with hundreds of tiny white or pale pink flowers in terminal heads. A number of these can be seen in the woods at the end of the Canaleta walk (Walk 24).

Another genus which cannot be ignored is *Euphorbia* or spurge of which Bonner says there are c.20 species in the Baleares. Only two are easy to identify however; the tree spurge *(Euphorbia dendroides)* which grows up to 2m high and is usually perfectly hemispherical with yellow glands surrounding the flowers, and *Euphorbia characias* a smaller, non-hemispherical plant with reddish-brown glands.

21

Beautiful specimens of these may be seen on the approach to Tomir by the old Binifaldo road (Walk 17b).

Two 'hedgehog' or 'pincushion' plants will be noticed by all walkers. Their sharp spines are an adaptation to wind as well as a protection against being eaten by grazing animals. These are *Teucrium subspinosum* and *Astralagus balearicus* and they are very difficult to tell apart when not in flower. In fact in Mallorquin they are both called *coixinets de monja* or 'nuns' sewing cushions'.

Smilax aspera or European sarsaparilla is a climbing plant with hooked spines on the stems, growing up through shrubs and hedges to 1-2m high. The leaves vary enormously in size according to the conditions, being very large in cool shady places and small and narrow in sunny ones. *Smilax balearica* is an endemic variety growing in the mountains. It has minimal leaves and is extremely prickly, becoming a great nuisance in places where it sometimes fills the crevices in otherwise bare limestone. Its backwards curving thorns are notorious for drawing blood and for tearing clothing and are one good reason for not wearing shorts on mountain walks.

One of the commonest mountain plants is *Ampelodesmus mauritanica*, a member of the grass family. This sometimes gives to distant hillsides the illusion of being the sort of sheep-cropped turf so familiar to British eyes. On closer inspection you find that there are enormous clumps of long thin leaves that grow quite tall before curving over to reach the ground, where the walker can step on them with one foot and then trip over them with the other. A sort of goose step is needed when walking on a narrow track through these grasses.

So far we have concentrated on the trees and shrubs and some other plants which make their presence obvious to the walker, but there are a number of smaller mountain plants which are well worth seeking out. A tiny plant, *Crocus minimus* shows its lilac-pink flowers before the leaves as early as December on the approach to the west top of Cavall Bernat (Walk 8) and in places along the ridge. The very common but delightful *Cyclamen balearicum* can be found in flower in March if you look for it under the sheltering leaves of other shrubs, both in woodland and on the mountains. The leaves, which are not unlike a house plant cyclamen, are a mottled greyish green and will be seen everywhere. They are a little like some other small plants which you will soon learn to recognise. One is Friar's cowl, *Arisarum vulgare*, which flowers in winter and the others are *Arum italicum, Arum pictum* and *Dranuculus muscivoros*. The latter is not common but is a very

Path to Coll d'es Coloms (Walks 23 & 24)

striking sight with a spotted reddish-purple 'spadix' and 'spathe' and strangely incised leaves. (A spadix is a fleshy spike bearing flowers and a spathe is a large bract enclosing the flower head.)

There is no space here to describe plants of other habitats such as the sea-coasts, the sand dunes, the cliff faces and the marshlands. For these the reader is referred to the books listed in the bibliography. Before beginning the next section though there are two very striking plants which must be mentioned although they are not native. One is the prickly pear, which is sometimes used as a dense protective hedge and whose fruits are edible, and the other is the *Agave americana*. This plant has huge leathery leaves which may be as long as 2m. After about ten years it sends up an enormous tree-like flower spike up to 10m high, after which it dies. Some will be seen near the airport, others cultivated in gardens.

Birds

These notes are written for walkers and not for experts, who again are referred to the books listed in the bibliography. Even those whose interest in birds is not very great are likely to find this interest stimulated by the number and variety of birds to be seen on nearly every walk. Binoculars and an identification book are a must. It so happens that some of the walks coincide with good birding areas e.g. Puig de Sa Roca Blanca (No.5) Atalaya de Albercuitx (6), Boquer valley (7), Castell del Rei (14), Puig Gros de Ternelles (15) and Tomir (17). There is a good chance of spotting interesting birds on many of the other walks too. In fact the only birds missed would be the ducks and waders, for which you would need to visit the northern marshes of Albufera or Albufereta, or the Salinas de Levante in the south-east. Details of these areas and the birds likely to be seen there will be found in Eddie Watkinson's book. (See p.142) Adverse weather conditions may bring in some interesting birds and a walk in these areas can be very rewarding at such times.

The hoopoe is a very common but extremely striking bird with its barred black and white wings and tail and its erectile crest. It is seen in many localities and will often be flushed out of the hedges as you drive along. Most exciting of all are the large birds of prey, especially the black vultures which may be seen soaring over the northern mountains such as Tomir and the Puig Gros de Ternelles.

There is a local birdwatching organisation on the island, the G.O.B. or Grupo Ornithologia Balear, based on Palma, which is very active.

Most local people however are more interested in shooting birds for the pot both in and out of the official season from the end of August to the end of January. Thrushes in fact can be a serious pest in the olive groves and *caza a coll* or thrush-netting is still allowed. Thrushes may be seen hanging up in bunches on market stalls. Many birds are protected by law and should you see any illegal shooting you can write to the G.O.B. at Calle Veri 1-3⁰ 2ª, Palma, with any evidence such as car number or photographs. All eagles, vultures, harriers, owls and flamingoes are protected. (Eddie Watkinson describes how he and others with the help of G.O.B. were successful in getting two men fined heavily for shooting a flamingo.)

The best time for birdwatchers to visit the island is the peak migration season in late April and May and the second choice would be September and October. July and August are poor for birds besides being too hot for serious walking, but all the winter months are good for both the resident population and the winter visitors.

Besides the resident black vultures, other raptors to be seen in winter are red kites, peregrines, kestrels and booted eagles, and more rarely the Golden Eagle and short-toed eagle. Marsh harriers are resident and breed on the larger marshes. Hen harriers and Montagu's harriers are occasional visitors. Osprey are frequently seen on the marshes and inland at the Gorg Blau and even at Boquer. One of the most interesting birds is the Eleanora's falcon which breeds in large colonies on the coastal cliffs all the way from Formentor to Dragonera island in the southwest. These birds arrive in late April but do not breed until later in the summer. The young birds then feed on tired migrants, an activity which may be observed during September and October in the nesting areas.

Other birds of the mountains include the fairly common crag martin which might be seen on Walk 26 (Castell d'Alaró) and in the Torrente de Pareis (Walk 21) and in many other places, including the marshes where flocks of about 1,000 may be seen catching insects on mild winter days.

Alpine accentors are seen in small flocks in the northern mountains, but we only saw a single one which shared our lunch on Massanella. The blue rock thrush is resident in fair numbers on mountains and coastal cliffs, but not easy to see in spite of its bright metallic blue plumage because of its tendency to disappear behind rocks as you catch a glimpse of it. Pallid swifts breed on the cliffs and small colonies of alpine swifts may be seen in a few places: the Artá peninsula, near the Puig Mayor and on the Castell del Rei walk.

In the woodlands the most common winter residents are blackcaps, black redstarts, crossbills and goldfinches. Also white wagtail, meadow pipit, hoopoes, serins and greenfinches, linnets and great tits are common and robins and chaffinches everywhere. Firecrests together with blackcaps are found as high as 800m. Rock doves are fairly common and nest on cliff faces, e.g. at Formentor, as well as in woods. Woodpigeons are not so common but may be seen on the Torrente de Pareis (Walk 21), on Galatzó (30) or in any of the oak woodlands on the approaches to the mountains.

The many areas of maquis and scrubland are the preferred habitats of a large number of birds including many warblers. The Sardinian warbler is a very common resident, as is the fantailed warbler. The Marmora's warbler is resident but somewhat elusive. It may be seen in the Boquer valley and Walk 5 (Puig de Sa Roca Blanca) passes the nesting sites on the way down to the Cases Veyas valley.

During the winter there is a big influx of birds from further north in Europe, including starlings, thrushes, finches, waders and wildfowl. Goldcrests are numerous and may outnumber the resident firecrests.

Other wildlife
Butterflies and moths abound in Mallorca and even midwinter there are always some to be seen. July and August are in fact the poorest months, apart from grasshoppers and cicadas, but again walkers are not likely to visit the island in these hottest months. Parrack (writing in 1973) mentions that 2,000 species of beetles have been listed and 32 butterflies plus 250 of the larger moths. The butterflies are the most striking and the most likely to be of interest to the general walker as opposed to the naturalist. Parrack classifies them into three groups: those widespread on the Continent, the Southern European or circum-Mediterranean group and those with only a sporadic Mediterranean distribution. The first group includes the red admiral which is one that is often seen in mild winter weather, and the clouded yellow and painted ladies which are more common in spring and the rare Camberwell beauty. The second group include some exotic species such as the two-tailed pasha which arrives in May from North Africa. Of the third group, the Mediterranean skipper is found from May onwards.

Other invertebrates include the shell-bearing molluscs, with the gastropods, or snails, being of particular interest. In the high mountains snails form the basic diet of the blue rock thrush and it has been noted that the colours of the shells vary in different areas and season by season. This colour variation is probably of survival value, depending on the colour of the background vegetation.

A large number of frogs live in the marshes and up to a height of 800m in the mountains. Many breed by the outlet from the Gorg Blau reservoir. Most of the frogs are an endemic form of the marsh frog, *Rana ridibunda*, but there is also a green tree frog, and three species of toad; the green toad, the natterjack and the midwife toad. They mostly hibernate in winter, but can be heard on a mild day at the Gorg Blau. There are four species of snake: grass snake, viperine snake, ladder snake and cowl snake, non of them being dangerous to man. They also hibernate from the end of October to April.

Two species of broad-toed lizards or geckos are found. The wall gecko lives mainly in lowland areas but it is the disc-fingered gecko which is more common in the mountains. The latter is the more bold of the two, but they both disappear quickly when approached. Both are eaten by the hoopoes. Although they hibernate, they come out sometimes on sunny winter days.

There are few large mammals on Mallorca due to two natural calamities since the severance of the island from the mainland c.800,000 years ago. The first of these was a rising of the water level with widespread flooding and the second was the climatic changes associated with the glaciations during the Quaternary. After this the final doom to a number of species was brought by man, not only as a hunter but as a destroyer of the forests through charcoal-burning and cultivation. The wild boar and the red fox probably survived until this century. The pine marten and the genet survive along with true wild cats, feral cats and weasels. Of the smaller mammals shrews, hedgehogs, bats, rabbits, the brown hare and various rodents are quite common. Rabbits provide food for man as well as the birds of prey who also do well off the smaller rodents.

The feral goats are the animals met with most frequently on mountain walks and the walker will often make use of the tracks they have made through the prickly scrub and the clumps of coarse *Ampelodesmus*. They are often the target for the many used cartridges the walker will notice in the Sierras.

From some of the cliff walks it is worth looking out to sea for whales and dolphins. There are occasional sightings of sperm whales and killer whales but mostly it is the common dolphin and sometimes the bottled-nosed and Risso's dolphin. Pilot whales are rare and rorquals more likely, both common rorqual and lesser rorqual. On rare occasions both have been beached on the island after heavy storms.

MAN AND HIS IMPACT ON THE LANDSCAPE

Mallorca was inhabited as long ago as 4,000 B.C. by men who made use of the many natural caves. Evidence for this was discovered in the 1960's when bones of extinct antelopes were found mingled with human remains in the Cueva de Muleta near Soller. Some 2,000 years later burial chambers were constructed, some of which can be seen near the west end of Cala San Vicente.

There are two major pre-historic sites on the island, one at Capacorp Vey (or Vell) near Lluchmayor and the other near Artá: the Talayot de Ses Paisses. The former is the most complete and can be visited by calling at the 500 year old farmhouse nearby for the key. There are two talayots, which are very ancient stone structures and the remains of a dozen houses.

The Romans invaded the island in 123 B.C. They built the cities of Palma and Alcudia (then known as Pollentia). The remains of the Roman town at Alcudia include the theatre on the road to Puerto Alcudia and other buildings near the Tucan cross-roads. In the Pollensa area there is a Roman bridge on the north side of the town, which can be seen easily when starting Walks 12, 13, 14 or 15. The remains of a Roman aqueduct are seen in the Ternelles valley, on Walks 14 and 15.

More striking and more numerous than the Roman remains are some of the mountain-top buildings that reflect Mallorca's long history of invasion and counter-invasion over the centuries. These are the defensive castles, such as the Castle del Rei and the Castle d'Alaró, which are seen on Walks 14 and 26, and also the *atalayas,* or watch-towers, placed in strategic positions to watch out for pirates or invaders. These towers are usually circular and can be climbed by iron rungs either inside or outside the walls to gain access to a viewing platform at the top. The Atalaya d'Alcudia is reached by Walks 2 and 3 and the Atalaya d'Albercuitx on Walk 6. The former is ruined but the latter almost complete.

Other buildings often found on the mountain tops are the *ermitas* or sanctuaries. Many of these offer a restaurant service, such as the Sanctuary of San Salvador near Felanitx, where the food is reputed to be very good. Some offer accommodation too, including one on the Puig de Maria near Pollensa, Walk 13.

It must be said that the most striking of all man-made structures on a mountain top is the radar station on the Puig Mayor. This unfortunate edifice can be seen from far too many places and is a too frequent reminder of the world today.

So far various buildings which may be encountered on some of the walks have been mentioned but the main aim in this chapter is to describe more extensive aspects of man's impact on the landscape. These will be dealt with under the headings of irrigation, cultivation and rural industries.

Irrigation

Mallorca is a very fertile island, considering that there is a very low rainfall, that there are no rivers and that most of the streams are dry for much of the year. Fortunately there is abundant water underground, occupying joints, solution holes and caverns in the limestone. This water has to stored in tanks and cisterns which will be observed everywhere alongside farms and smallholdings. So also will the *seguias* or open channels, carrying water along into the fields and terraces.

Even more noticeable are the windmills used to pump up water from wells on the central plain, now mainly replaced by electric pumps with the windmill serving as a support for a TV aerial. Occasionally you will see a *noria*, or water-wheel. These were introduced by the Arabs, along with the *seguias*, and used to pump up the well-water before they were replaced by the windmills or by electric pumps.

Cultivation

The Arabs also introduced the terracing supported by dry stone walls which is another aid to cultivation, making it easier to work the land as well as preventing erosion.

One of the most impressive sights in Mallorca is the blossoming of the almond trees in early spring when a large part of the island becomes pink and white. There are said to be over six million almond trees today and most of the crop is exported. Planting of the almonds began in 1765, but the olive tree has been cultivated for much longer, possibly for a thousand years or more. Some of these very old trees with gnarled and twisted trunks will be seen on terraces on many of the mountain walks.

Orange trees too are another sight to delight and interest the walker. There appears to be ripe fruit on some of the trees all the year round, but the main crop is ripe in January. Soller is famous for its orange groves, but they can be seen in many other parts of the island too, for example in the *huertas* or market gardens near Pollensa on the way to the Ternelles valley in Walks 14 and 15.

Potatoes are another major crop grown for export, but these will not be seen on any of the walks as they are cultivated in the flat area near Inca. Vines are grown here, near Binisalem and near Felanitx in the south. Some very good wine is made in both these areas.

Fresh vegetables are grown all the year round, thanks to the sunshine and the irrigation system, and it is a delight to look into gardens in the depths of winter and see lettuces and other salad crops ready for picking. One Englishman we met, living in Puerto Pollensa, was reluctantly going to England in late December, but looking forward to harvesting some peas he had just planted, when he returned in February.

Some of the methods of cultivation used date back for thousands of years and are in themselves a pleasure to watch. Horses and mules pull a primitive plough along the narrow terraces, where catch-crops will be grown between fruit trees. Imported machinery is very expensive, and in any case it is much easier to manage an animal than a machine in these places. Some of the terraces on steep ground could not be reached by a tractor. A man may be observed sowing seed by scattering it from a sack tied around his neck, looking like a biblical illustration.

Rural Industries

There are two major 'rural industries', the remains of which will be seen time and time again on many walks in this book. In fact, they are intimately connected with these walks because many of the footpaths the walker uses were made by the workers in these activities i.e. charcoal-burning and snow collecting. Knowing something about these adds greatly to the interest of the walks.

(a). Charcoal burning

The most extensive remains are of the charcoal-burning sites. On almost every walk that goes through an evergreen oak forest these flat circular areas will be noticed, often ringed by stones and covered with bright green moss. Many have been pointed out as a landmark in the route descriptions. They are known as *sitjes* (singular *sitja*), a Mallorquin word which is sometimes roughly translated as fireplace, but the real English equivalent of which would be 'pitstead' or 'charcoal pitstead'. The production of charcoal in Mallorca continued until butane gas became popular in the 1920's. Its only use was for cooking, preferred rather than wood because it gives a cleaner and steadier heat.

The charcoal burners began work in April and lived and worked all summer in the woods with their families. They could not leave the site because charcoal-burning is a delicate operation and everything could be ruined in a moment of neglect. For this reason they built huts to live in, the remains of which may sometimes be found in the woods, often with an old oven nearby in which they used to bake bread. (Walks 23, 24 and 29).

The process of making the charcoal began with the felling of large oaks, of a diameter stipulated by the landowner. Each *carbonero* had his own area known as a *ranxo**. Axes and enormous two-handed saws were used to fell the trees. Meanwhile a perfectly flat and circular site had to be prepared. Stones were carefully arranged so that sufficient circulation of air would carbonise the wood without igniting it. On this platform the cut logs and branches were arranged in a 'cupola', leaving a narrow central chimney. Over all this was arranged a covering of gravel and clay. A ladder was needed to reach the central chimney through which the *carbonero* dropped live coals to start the process, and to feed the fire from time to time with small pieces of dry wood. Constant vigilance and expertise were needed on the part of the worker.

During the process the weight of the wood was reduced by 75-80%. Each firing lasted for 10 to 12 days, and would produce around 2,800 kilograms. When the operation was completed the covering was removed and very hot pieces extracted with a shovel and rake. Sieved earth was used for quenching as water caused a loss of quality. Finally the charcoal was sorted into a number of different grades and taken by muleteers for sale at special shops in the villages. Bark from the oak trees was also collected and used for tanning.

A fine reconstruction of a charcoal-burning structure can be seen on the Son Moragues estate in walk 29.

(b)   Snow collecting
The charcoal-burning sites are found at various heights but always of course below the tree-line, whereas the *casas de nieve,* or snow houses are always high up in the mountains. Snow was collected to make ice and conserved in these unique structures, many of which will be seen

*a ranxo = 4 cuarteradas. 1 cuarterada = c.75 square feet.   31

on the mountain walks e.g. on Tomir and Massanella, Walks 17 and 22. Most of them are pits rather than 'houses', some circular and some rectangular, either wholly or partially below ground level and sometimes roofed over.

In winter when the mountains were covered with snow, groups of men from the nearest villages went up to gather the snow in carriers and baskets made of cane or grass. To make collecting easier flat platforms were often made and cleared of vegetation. These can still be seen near the pits. Here the snow was arranged in layers and trampled down hard to pack it into ice, while entoning the following rhyme:

> ★*pitgen sa neu, pitgen sa neu*
> *i tots estan dins ses cases*
> *peguen potades, peguen potades*
> *en Toni, en Xisco, en Juan i N'Andreu*

> ★'tramp the snow, tramp the snow
> and throw it in the shed
> earn the bread, earn the bread
> for Tony, Harry, John and Joe'

The packed snow was put in the pit and each layer covered with a thin layer of reed-grass (to make it easier to extract blocks when required). When the pit was full, it was protected with a layer of ashes and finally a thick covering of branches. One man remained on duty all the year to maintain the covering in perfect condition. In the summer nights, huge blocks of snow/ice were taken on muleback to the villages and towns. It was not only used for ice-creams and such, but also medicinally. An emulsion with olive-oil was used for dressing wounds and was believed to stop bleeding.

The local authority controlled the price and limited the production of ice, supposedly to prevent speculation. There was a specific tax on it. Sometimes snow had to be imported from Cataluña by boat, but in other years there was overproduction and snow was exported to Menorca. It appears that the last occasion in which a snow-pit was used was in 1925 on the Puig de Massanella. The *casa de nieve* on Son Moragues was built in the seventeenth century, but it was never a major one as its altitude was not sufficiently high and it was abandoned in the eighteenth century. Nearby, the hut where the *nevaters* or snow-workers lived has been made into a shelter for walkers.

There were in all some twenty or more of these *casas de nieve* in the mountains of Mallorca, most of them at an altitude of over 900m.

(c). *Lime-burning*

Brief mention must be made of the lime kilns which will be seen from time to time. There are three of them in the Cairats valley on Son Moragues, Walk 29. They are rather different from those seen in the British Isles in that they are normally cylindrical. Lime is used for whitening houses, something which used to be done every year, and also for making mortar and cement in the construction industry. Great heat is needed to initiate the reaction $CaCO_3 \rightarrow CaO + CO_2$, so these *hornos de calc* were always built near a plentiful supply of wood. Great destruction of woodland was often the result. Although almost all the rock on Mallorca is limestone, stones used to convert to lime were chosen very carefully, but always from somewhere close at hand. They were known as *piedra viva* or living stones.

From the base of the circular pit used as a kiln, a cupola was built up of large stones with spaces left between them so that the flames could pass through. Above the cupola the rest of the oven was built up of stones and finally covered with slaked lime and soil. The interior of the cupola was filled with wood and the fire lit. It was kept burning for a period varying from nine to fifteen days, wood being thrown in continually. The quantity required is impressive: up to 10 tons of branches during one firing. A firing would produce around 100-150 tons of lime. It was hard work, the fire needing to be fed by day and night, nor were the financial rewards very high according to the old saying *'Qui fa calc, va descalc'*, (He who makes lime goes barefoot).

CISTUS ALBIDUS

WALKING IN MALLORCA

Equipment and clothing

Although the winters in Mallorca are normally mild and the weather is ideal for walking, bad weather is not unknown as in any area of high mountains. There are days when you will be glad of a warm sweater, anorak, hat, gloves and waterproofs, especially on the higher mountains when you should always be prepared for a possible deterioration in the conditions. There will also be days when you can walk in shirt-sleeves even in January, the coldest month. Boots are advised for most of walks, although those graded 'C' could be done in trainers or strong shoes if preferred. If it is very warm and you prefer to wear shorts, at least take long trousers or breeches in your rucsac, not only to allow for a change in the conditions but because of the prickly vegetation encountered on so many walks. Sunglasses and a sunhat might be welcome or even necessary in the spring or autumn as well as the summer. The heat also means that you may get dehydrated and it is advisable to carry drinks. Fruit juices are available in small cartons and cans almost everywhere and the cheap fresh fruit, especially the oranges are very thirst quenching.

Snow does fall on the high tops most years, but it is very rare for it to fall at sea level as it did in December and January 1984-5. When this happens, the roads to the mountains are cut off for days on end, not only by snow but by fallen trees. The snow is likely to be wet and soft too, so that ice axes and crampons can be left at home, unless it is intended to seek out the snow.

This book deals only with walks and occasional scrambles, none of which require a rope. The whole island abounds in steep rock however and should give good climbing on secluded crags and cliffs to anyone interested.

Of other standard walking equipment take a whistle, compass and torch. Darkness falls early in winter (about 17.30 on the shortest days) so that you may need a torch if you are late back from a walk.

Maps

The best map for getting about the island is the Firestone map, BALEARES: Map Turistico, scale 1:125,000. This is available at petrol stations, newsagents and some general stores throughout the island. (Price 250 pta. in 1985). Other general maps can be very inaccurate indeed and are not worth buying.

There are no ordnance survey maps of the high standard of the British O.S. maps or the French I.G.N. maps. The nearest equivalent are the military maps *(mapas militares)* on a scale of 1:50,000 and 1:25,000. These are available from Stanfords' International Map Centre at 14 Long Acre, London and can also be bought in Palma from the Libreria Fondevila at 12 & 14 Calle Arabi. The three most important maps for walkers are Pollensa, Soller and Inca all on the 1:50,000 scale and the next three are Formentor, Aucana and Artá also 1:50,000. References to the appropriate maps are given at the beginning of each walk description. They are worth having in spite of inaccuracies. It is much cheaper to buy maps on the island than in London, but it takes time to get into Palma and find the shop. For a short stay holiday it is better to buy maps before setting out in order to have the maximum time for walking. If you want to go into Palma and do not like the idea of driving and parking, then a good plan is to take the 'Pont d'Inca' road instead of the motorway by forking left at the junction 10km to the north of the city. Keep going straight on through several sets of traffic lights until a large SEAT* building is seen on the right. There is free parking here and taxis pass every few minutes showing a green *libre* sign. Ask for the Plaza España, which is a good place from which to explore Palma. It is a large square where many buses stop and where the trains leave for Inca and Soller. There is a street plan of Palma on the reverse of the Firestone Map which can be used to find your way around.

When using the *mapas militares* to explore the mountains, remember that the terrain is frequently more complex than indicated by the map. For example, steep cliffs are not always shown, new roads have been built and old ones fallen into disuse. Always leave time to get back to the starting point by the same way in case of unexpected difficulties.

Grading definitions

All the walks in this book have been done by the writer. An attempt has been made to assess the difficulties in such a way that anyone using the book can form a reasonable idea of what to expect. Such assessment is obviously very subjective and can also be influenced by the weather conditions at the time and many other factors. When heavy rain occurs then the normally dry stream beds can become 'torrents' in the English sense of the word and paths can be running with swift water. At these times it is obviously better to keep away from any walks involving such objective dangers. Fortunately conditions like this do not normally last very long and all the excess

*SEAT (pronounced SAY-AT) is the Spanish version of FIAT

water quickly disappears into the limestone.

Assuming normal conditions then, the walks have been graded into three categories which can be called difficult, average and easy, or A, B and C. Note that these gradings have nothing to do with the length of the walk and the approximate distances. Times and heights involved are given in addition to the grading at the beginning of each walk description.

A   A difficult walk, often pathless in parts, with considerable route-finding and/or some scrambling. Normally only to be attempted by experienced walkers.

B   An average mountain walk which may call for some skill in route-finding.

C   Easy walking along well-defined paths or tracks and with no route-finding difficulties.

Sometimes these grades have been qualified by a + sign to indicate a slightly greater degree of difficulty than the above definitions, not sufficient to warrant the next higher grade.

The walking times given allow time to stop for photographs and to look at flowers and birds etc., but do not include long stops for refreshments or rests. On the whole they are for slower than average walkers. Much of the terrain however is rough going and often takes longer to negotiate than expected.

Access
Many of the walks in this book go across privately-owned land. The maps do not show rights of way. However, by Spanish law there is a right of way on any track leading to the sea, to a mountain top, or to monasteries, hermitages, towers or other famous landmarks, which just about covers every walk. Certainly land-owners are friendly and helpful, even on occasion going out of their way to point out a path. On the other hand we once met a Mallorquin who told us he had been denied access to land near the *finca* Fartaritx del Raco (Walk 18.) This man, walking with his family, said he had been walking regularly on the island for 25 years and this was the first time such a thing had happened.

Another fact worth knowing is that the ubiquitous sign *coto privado de caza* only means 'private hunting' and can be ignored by walkers. (The black and white rectangular sign means the same: sometimes these are useful where they occur on land boundaries in rough terrain with no other landmarks).

Many tracks have a standard 'no entry' sign which means that cars are prohibited, but there is nothing to stop walkers. Often an access gate or stile is provided when the gate is a locked one. On the other hand there are some private estates where walkers would be distinctly unwelcome, like one on the Aucanada peninsula we came to when exploring for this book. A ten-foot high iron gate, heavily padlocked and topped by iron spikes, with fences either side of similar height and crowned with barbed wire spelt out an obvious message; we turned back and found another walk.

There is no access to the summit of the Puig Mayor, the highest mountain on the island, because it is occupied by a military radar station. The western spur of the Puig Mayor, the Penyal de Mig Dia, is outside the boundary of the radar station, but nevertheless special permission is required to climb it. At one time there was a popular annual excursion to see the sunrise from here, replacing an even more popular excursion to the Puig Mayor itself before the radar station was built. A long walk was made of it, starting from Biniaraitx near Soller and descending to Fornalutx, giving an ascent of 1,233m and including some difficult route-finding on the descent. However, I am informed by the President of the *Federácion de Montanismo* that at the present time (1985) such permission is not being granted. Should this situation change, then the following brief description may be useful:

Leave the C710 by the bridge 300m west of the tunnel and go steeply up towards the Coll de N'Arbona. The col is in the military zone, so just before reaching it go up to the left towards the summit. It is best to aim for the ridge to the north, a little to the right of the actual summit. (This is steep ground and can be dangerous in snow.) From the top (1,385m) follow the ridge to another top at 1,343m which is the one seen from the valley. Continue to follow the ridge down to the Aries Spur until a way can be found down to the right (north) to reach the Bini valley. (This is not easy and should not be attempted in mist; better to descend the way you have come in bad weather.) Once in the Bini valley turn left along the track over the Coll d'es Carcoles and then take a left fork to return to the main road.

Use either the Soller 1:50,000 or the Soller 1:25,000, but note that the latter does not show the new road.

Walkers 'country code'
It goes without saying that all walkers should have the utmost respect for the countryside through which they walk and for the people who

live or work there. This means that all gates should be left as found, care should be taken not to frighten animals or damage crops, flowers should not be picked, fires should not be started and all litter should be taken back to your hotel.

ICONA

This is the national institute for nature conservation. (El Instituto National para la Conservacion de la Naturaleza.) They are doing a lot of good work on the island and have acquired several tracts of land which are being conserved for public use, constructed some excellent paths (and signposted them) and provided some well-equipped picnic sites with shelters, cooking facilities and toilets.

One of their largest undertakings is the purchase of the Son Moragues estate near Valldemossa which has become an open-air museum with reconstructions of charcoal-burning sites etc., and ICONA have published a walking guide to this. (See bibliography, and Walk 29.) Other areas are the Gorg Blau (Walk 23 & 24) and the Coll Baix - Pena Roca area (Walk 2 & 3).

Mountain Rescue

If you wish to take out insurance for rescue costs then it is probably best to arrange this through the B.M.C. scheme, or one of the other special insurance schemes before your holiday. An alternative is to apply for a climbing permit *(Licencia)* from the Federación Balear de Montanismo. The address is Pere Alcantara Pena 13 in Palma and the office is open on Tuesdays and Fridays from 7.30 a.m. until 8.30 p.m. You need to have with you a membership card from a mountaineering club in order to obtain a permit. If you are not in such a club then it is possible to join the Grup Excursionista Mallorca (Calle Impremta 1, -2° 07001 Palma de Mallorca). The cost of this (1985) is 1,500pta per annum and includes insurance, information, use of club facilities and the opportunity to join organised excursions. There may be an additional charge for the *Licencia.*

In the event of an accident in the mountains the first people to contact are the Guardia Civil. (Tel. 46-51-12). If the injured person has a *Licencia* then the police should be informed. A report *(Parte de Accidente)* will have to be made out by an officer of the G.E.M. or the Federación in order to claim the costs.

Guide

There is an experienced Mallorquin guide living in Puerto Pollensa who can take parties rock-climbing, caving or walking in any part of the island. He speaks fluent English and French. His name is Mauricio Espinar and the address is Calle Almirante Cervera, 23 Puerto de Pollensa, Mallorca. (Tel. 53-10-30).

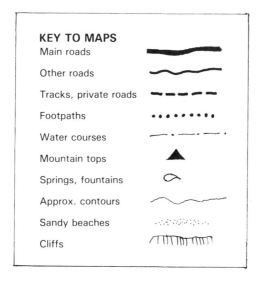

KEY TO MAPS

Main roads	
Other roads	
Tracks, private roads	
Footpaths	
Water courses	
Mountain tops	
Springs, fountains	
Approx. contours	
Sandy beaches	
Cliffs	

Mallorca

Map 1. Location of Walks

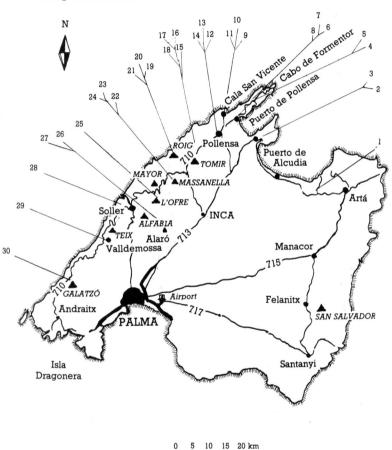

Mountains and tops over 1000m

The heights are those given on the military maps and the figures in brackets are alternative heights from the 1985 Firestone map or from the book by Palos (see p.141). The criteria for separate mountain status are a separation of 1km or over and/or a re-ascent of 100m or more.

Mountains	Tops	Height	Comments
1. Puig Mayor	Main top Mitx Dia West top P. de Ses Vinyes	1443 (1445) 1385 1343 1103 (1101)	In military zone. Outside military zone. but permission required.
2. Massanella	Main top Twin top Unnamed tops west P.de Ses Bassetas P.Galileu Sa Mola Es Fronto (west) Es Fronto (east)	1352 (1349) 1348 1255, 1233, 1061 1215 1195 1159 1055 1015	An enormous massif consisting of two long curving ridges sep. by two valleys leading to the high Coll d'es Prat. (The old pilgrims' route from Soller to Lluch).
3. Tossals Vert	Main top S.top P.des Nogue Morro d'Almallutx Tossals	1115 1103 1074 1059 1047 (1048)	The Tossals group is S. of Gorg Blau & E. of Cuber.
4. Sa Rateta	Main top Unnamed top to S.W.	1107 1060	On ridge to L'Ofre.
5. Tomir	Main top S.W. top	1102 (1103) 1070	Dominates Pollensa valley.
6. L'Ofre		1090	1.8km from Sa Rateta.
7. Alfabia	Main top Palou 'Antennae' top P.d'es Coll des Jou	1067 (1068) 1042 1034 1046	Main top of long ridge. 1km N.E. of Alfabia. 2.1km S.W. of Alfabia. 0.5km S.E. of Palou. (offset from main ridge).
8. Teix	Main top East top Canizo	1063 1062 1004	Between Deià & Valldemosa. 0.75km to north of main tops.
9. P.de N'Alis		1038	Divided from Massanella massif by Coll de Sa Linea.
10. Galatzó		1026 (1025)	Highest peak in S.E. of Mallorca.
11. Cornadors		1009	1.6km N.E. of Alfabia.
12. Puig Roig		1002	Most northerly 1000m peak.

Weathered limestone (Walk 16)

ROUTE
DESCRIPTIONS

Map 2. Walk 1. Bec de Faruch

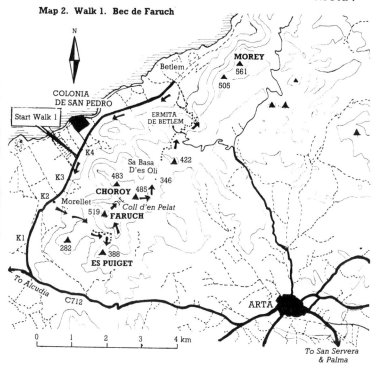

1. FARUCH, OR BEC DE FERRUTX

Although the Artà mountains are only of the order of 500m they have all the characteristics of the higher mountains of the Sierra de Tramuntana and in places are even more wild. The Bec de Ferrutx is a spectacular shape and this interesting walk has good views in all directions.

Starting point:	Colonia de San Pedro.
Time:	6hr.
Distance:	14.5km.
Height:	519m.
Grade:	B+
Map:	Artà 1:50,000

There is ample space for parking at K3.7 on the road to Betlem where there is a wide road junction. Walk back along the road to Morellet, a house partly hidden by trees, and turn up left by the stream just before reaching the house, keeping as close to it as possible. The orchard next to the stream has been ploughed very close to this edge, so look out for a place where you can cross the stream to reach a field track on the other bank. At the end of the cultivated ground re-cross the stream and make for a gate opening on to a rough area where a wide track can be followed for a short distance. This very soon disappears and it is a question of picking your own way up to the low saddle ahead. A gap in the wall across the valley can be found on the right hand side of the stream bed between two small hillocks. This part of the walk is a little tedious, but once the saddle is reached a narrow path develops on the left, rising gradually and cutting back into two side valleys. Eventually it reaches the col between the Bec de Ferrutx and Es Puiget above a prominent rock band. At the col turn left and follow the subsidiary ridge up until it joins the main mass of the mountain, where bear left again to reach the summit. There is a rather ugly roofless shelter near the trig point, which is reached some 200m from the highest point of the ridge.

From the trig point, drop down easy ground to the Coll d'en Pelat (416m), near which is a solitary pine tree, and continue in the same direction to the Puig d'en Choroy (485m), arriving first at a small saddle and turning right to reach the small marker stone on the top. All this area is stony and arid with a garigue type of vegetation: many asphodels, flat-topped thistles, sparse clumps of *ampelodesmus* grass and some dwarf fan palms. From the top of Choroy, a ridge drops down in an easterly direction at first, curving round to the north to lead to a little plain, the Basa d'es Oli where there are many heaps of stones. A small path (marked on the map) can then be picked up, but soon becomes confused with a new track (not marked on the map). After rising over a small shoulder this track can be left at the point where it makes a sharp right turn, keeping in roughly the same direction as before. The old path can be picked up a little lower down after finding your way down a small escarpment. Although little used, this path can be followed easily to the Ermita de Betlem, where an asphalted road arrives from Artá. This road makes a 180° turn here and is followed down for 100m to a fountain, signposted 'Fuente'. Opposite the fountain, which is roofed over and provided with a chained iron ladle, there is a gateway to a wide track which soon doubles back and leads down the valley towards Betlem. This path is not on the map. This is still a very beautiful valley although a forest fire has destroyed the trees in the upper part. The path leads to the only possible way down a steep head wall and can be followed until it disappears into a ploughed field. Here turn left and pick up another track which leads to the road, keeping a stone wall on the left. Easy walking back along the road to the starting point, with fine views across the bay.

San Pedro junction - Trig point	2hr. 15min.
Trig point - top of Choroy	40min.
Choroy - Ermita de Betlem	1hr.10min.
Ermita - San Pedro junction	2hr.

2. PEÑA ROCA AND ATALAYA DE ALCUDIA

An easy walk mainly along good paths built and maintained by ICONA, with excellent views. There is a shelter on the Atalaya with a well on the flat terrace outside.

Leave Alcudia on the Mal Pas road by going straight on at the first traffic lights coming from the Puerto Pollensa direction. This is a narrow road and slightly off-set so that you have to do a right then a left turn. Follow the coast road, turning right after approx. 4km to the *Ermita* where there is a large parking area.

Starting point:	Ermita de la Victoria.
Time:	3hr.
Distance:	6km.
Height:	355m, 444m.
Grade:	C+.
Map:	Aucana 1:25,000 or Cabo Formentor 1:50,000.

Go up past the buildings by a wide track which makes a sharp bend to the right in about 20min. The Peña Roca path begins just round this corner and is signposted. It is a most attractive path which contours along the base of the crags and eventually rounds the end of the ridge by a roofed-over section to reach a couple of old stone shelters. One of these is very curious, the only access being through a hole in the roof. From here, a rough steep path leads up in about 10min. to the top of the Peña Roca, where the barrel of an old cannon still lies on the flat circular top. This has at one time been walled, and also floored with cobbles.

Map 3.
Walk 2. **Pena Roca and the Atalaya de Alcudia**
Walk 3. **Atalaya de Alcudia by Fontanelles**

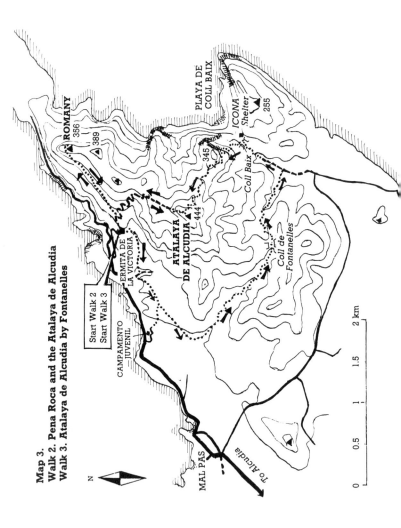

Return by the same way to the wide track and turn left along it, up to a broad col at 315m. From here a narrow but well built path with a protective handrail leads steeply to the Atalaya de Alcudia. Just before the top, by the Ermita signpost, will be seen the very good path descending to the Coll Baix which is used as a route of ascent in Walk 3. The shelter is on the south side of the top and the views from the terrace are splendid.

Ermita - - Peña Roca	1hr.5min.
Pena Roca - Atalaya de Alcudia	1hr.15min.
Atalaya de Alcudia - Ermita	40min.

3. ATALAYA DE ALCUDIA BY FONTANELLES

This walk makes use of a very good but disused footpath up the Fontanelles valley and over the Coll de Fontanelles to the forest road on the south side of the Atalaya. An excellent ICONA path then leads from the Coll Baix, where there is a shelter and a water supply, to the Atalaya. A diversion can be made from the Coll Baix to a small sandy beach, the Playa de Coll Baix.

Starting point:	Ermita de la Victoria.
Time:	4hr.
Distance:	9km.
Height:	444m.
Grade:	B.
Map:	Aucana 1:25,000 or Cabo Formentor 1:50,000.

Leave Alcudia by the road to Malpas and park at the Ermita as for Walk 2. The walk begins by a small stone building near the point where the forest track rises up behind the old *Ermita* building. The start is not obvious, but after dropping steeply down for a short distance a good path will be found leading down to a stream bed. This is crossed and recrossed and eventually joined before reaching a cross-track. Turn right along this and after 200m strike up left by a rough shelter to join another track going up to the left. Follow this through some newly planted trees until it joins a track coming from the Campamento de la Victoria (a children's holiday place with tennis courts and playing fields). Turn left and follow the track in a big swing round to the right to reach the Fontanelles valley. Here the old but disused path is picked up. Although slightly overgrown it is easy to follow and continues right up to the col.

At the col two paths will be seen. Take the left hand one, which leads down through a narrow wooded valley to meet a forest road at a T-junction. Turn left and in about 15 minutes the Coll Baix will be reached. The path to the beach begins on the far side of the shelter, and the path up to the Atalaya rises up through the trees on the north-west side of the col. This path passes close to the top of the Puig des Boc which is a good viewpoint, before going on to the top of the Atalaya with its shelter and well.

From the summit return to the signpost and go straight on down the steep well-constructed path to a wide col, from where a forest track goes down to the *Ermita*.

Ermita - Campamento path	40min.
Campamento path - Coll des Fontanelles	50min.
Coll des Fontanelles - Coll Baix	40min.
Coll Baix - Atalaya de Alcudia	1hr.10min.
Atalaya de Alcudia - Ermita	40min.

4. EL FUMAT AND ROCA BLANCA

The Fumat is a spectacular peak which overhangs the Formentor road near the tunnel. This short excursion is mainly pathless but not difficult and on a good day the views are excellent. The route makes use of an old track which was used to reach the lighthouse before the new road was constructed in 1968.

Starting point:	Mirador near K15, Formentor road
Time:	2hr.35min.
Distance:	4km.
Height:	334m and 337m
Grade:	B.
Map:	Cabo Formentor 1:25,000.

Walk back along the road towards the tunnel and scramble up the hillside to reach the old lighthouse track which is just above the new road at a point marked by a cairn. Follow this narrow track which leads up to the col between El Fumat and Roca Blanca at a very easy gradient. The top of the Fumat is reached quite easily from this col, up rock slabs and stony ground at an easy angle. Descend the same way to the col and go up the ridge ahead to the Roca Blanca. There is

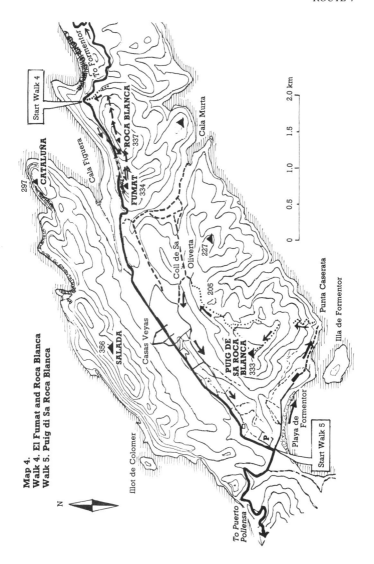

Map 4.
Walk 4. El Fumat and Roca Blanca
Walk 5. Puig di Sa Roca Blanca

49

Roca Blanca (Walk 4)

no path here but there are no difficulties. From the last top on the ridge continue downwards in the same direction, avoiding steep rocks when necessary on the south side. The ridge ends in a short cliff, but an easy way down can be found leading back to the right.

From here walk along to the foot of the cliff, then make for the large pine tree in the valley below. Follow the red earth path back to the Mirador.

Mirador - El Fumat	45min.
El Fumat - col	15min.
Col - first top Roca Blanca	25min.
First top - last top	25min.
Last top - Mirador	45min.

5. PUIG DE SA ROCA BLANCA

A short, easy walk, mainly on paths, except for the first part of the descent which is a little rough and stony. The top overlooks the colourful waters near the Formentor beach and on a clear day there are views across to the Alcudia hills and beyond them to Artá. The return route passes the nesting-sites of the Marmora's warblers and goes through the sheltered, wooded valley near the Casas Veyas where migrant birds rest during the spring and autumn migrations. During the winter this is a good place for resident birds such as hoopoes, black redstarts, firecrests, crossbills, linnets and great tits.

Starting point:	Formentor car park.
Time:	3hr.20min.
Distance:	8km.
Height:	333m.
Grade:	C+.
Map:	Pollensa & Cabo Formentor 1:50,000 or Cala San Vicens and Cabo Formentor, 1:25,000.

Walk along the sea front, past the front of the Formentor Hotel after which the road turns inland. (The grounds are private but there is a right of way between hotel and the sea. If you go behind the hotel, the road is on the left after passing the tennis courts.) Take the second road on the right, which ends at a new house on the Punta Caserata. Turn left up the steep hillside between a stream bed and the locked gate to this house, keeping fairly near the fence. This is rough going at first, but in five minutes an old neglected path will be reached. This zig-zags upwards and is easy to follow at first. Eventually it goes off to the right and at this point it must be avoided. Instead, keep going upwards in the same general line until a more definite path is again found, leading easily up the south ridge to the summit.

From the top follow the ridge down in a north-easterly direction to join a path at an unnamed col. A few cairns mark the way, which keeps fairly close to the edge of some steep ground on the left. Follow the path along to the Coll de Sa Oliverta and then down into the wooded valley below. Ignore the first turning left which goes above the trees, but take the left fork at the junction reached about ten minutes after leaving the col, then another left fork after a further ten minutes. Ignore a right turn leading to the road and continue to a flat sportsfield, the 'Campo de Desportes, Formentor'. Cross the field at its left hand edge to find a track leading to the right. After 100m fork left at a minor cross-track and follow this down to the car park.

Formentor car park - Puig de Sa Roca Blanca	1hr.50min.
Puig de Sa Roca Blanca - Coll de Sa Oliverta	40min.
Coll de Sa Oliverta - Formentor car park	50min.

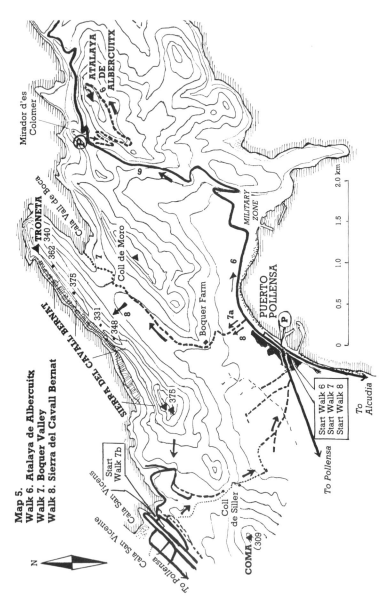

Map 5.
Walk 6. Atalaya de Albercuitx
Walk 7. Boquer Valley
Walk 8. Sierra del Cavall Bernat

N

ATALAYA DE ALBERCUITX

Mirador d'es Colomer

6

9

MILITARY ZONE

TRONETA

Cala Vall de Boca

340

362

375

Coll de Moro

7

331

348

8

375

SIERRA DEL CAVALL BERNAT

Boquer Farm

7a

6

PUERTO POLLENSA

P

8

0   0.5   1.0   1.5   2.0 km

To Alcudia

| Start Walk 6 |
| Start Walk 7 |
| Start Walk 8 |

To Pollensa

Start Walk 7b

Cala San Vicens

To pollensa

Cala San Vicente

Coll de Siller

COMA (309)

52

6. ATALAYA DE ALBERCUITX

This is a very easy walk with splendid views. Although a large part of it is on a road, this road is a quiet one in winter especially if weekends are avoided. As it starts in Puerto Pollensa it can be done by anyone without a car, and since it goes through the trees and scrub near the Albercuitx Farm there is a good chance of seeing some interesting birds. An alternative if a car is available would be to park at the Mirador d'es Colomer, from where it is only about 1hr.30min. to the Atalaya and back, and then go on to do either Walk 4 or Walk 5 further along the Formentor peninsula.

Starting point:	Puerto Pollensa.
Time:	4hr.15min.
Distance:	14km.
Height:	380m.
Grade:	C.
Map:	Pollensa 1:50,000, or Pollensa 1:25,000 & Cala Sant Vicens 1:25,000.

From the Puerto walk along the sea front as far as possible then turn left to reach the Formentor road. Follow this up to the Mirador d'es Colomer, where it is worth going out along the short path for the view down to the detached rock 'El Colomer' and across the sea to the Cala Vall de Boquer, where the steep rocks at the end of the Cavall Bernat ridge dip into the sea. Opposite the Mirador carpark, go up the road which was built to reach a former barracks high up near the Atalaya. It soon leads round to the other side of the hill with views of Formentor passing, on the left, a tunnel about 200m. long leading to an old ammunition store. This is quite safe to investigate if you have a torch, provided no one drops anything down the two vertical shafts at the end of the tunnel.

The track continues past the old barracks and then makes a sharp turn left back towards the highest buildings. From here a narrow path goes up to the old watch tower. This can be climbed by means of iron rungs cemented into the outside wall and leading into an upper chamber. From the chamber, rungs on the inside lead to a viewing platform at the top where the views are really spectacular. Part of the parapet round the platform is missing, so care is needed.

The return is by the same way, but it is possible to vary it slightly by going down the ridge that lies roughly parallel to the road, leaving the

53

Atalaya d'Albercuitx (Walk 6)

barracks track where it makes a sharp bend round the end of this ridge and rejoining the road at K3.6, where there is a sharp bend just by an electricity pylon. This ridge is rough walking with no path but is not steep; it would be graded either C+ or B, so if an easy walk is wanted it is better to return to the Mirador and back down the road.

Puerto - Mirador d'es Colomer	1hr.30min.
Mirador - Atalaya de Albercuitx	1hr. (includes tunnel)
Atalaya - Mirador	30min.
Mirador - Puerto	1hr.15min.

7. BOQUER VALLEY

(a) From Puerto Pollensa

A very easy and attractive walk through this sheltered valley much favoured by migrant birds. It is also interesting botanically and the flowers of *cyclamen balearicum* can be found within a few feet of the valley wall, not far from the Boquer farm just near a water source on the right hand side (seen as early as 20 March in 1985). There is a good path right down to the coast at the small shingly beach of Cala Boquer, where the Cavall Bernat ridge ends very steeply and there are views across to the detached rock of Colomer.

Starting point:	Puerto de Pollensa.
Time:	2hr.
Distance:	6km.
Height:	101m.
Grade:	C.
Map:	Cala San Vicens 1:25,000 and Pollensa 1:25,000 or Pollensa 1:50,000.

If arriving by car, turn left where the Pollensa road meets the sea front and park just here; there are always plenty of parking spaces in winter at least. Walk along the sea-front to the left and go straight on along a footpath in front of a terrace of small hotels. Turn left along the Avenida Bocharis at the end of this terrace and cross the main Formentor road exactly opposite the stone gateposts of the entrance to the Boquer farm track. Follow this to the farm and pass in front of the farmhouse to go through the iron gate at the end of the courtyard.

Boquer Valley (Walks 7 & 8)

Turn right immediately, go through another gate and follow the track between some immense boulders into the Boquer valley. The valley is bounded on the north-west by the splendid Cavall Bernat ridge in which the spectacular hole reached on Walk 8 will be observed. The track passes through gaps in the stone walls and over the low Coll de Moro, from where it continues as a narrower path down to the sea. Unfortunately the tiny beach is usually spoiled by debris washed in by the sea, but it is possible to walk on past a fisherman's shelter to a small platform overlooking the bay. Return is by the same way.

(b) From Cala San Vicente

Walkers staying at Cala San Vicente can get to Puerto Pollensa by bus, or else walk over the Coll de Siller, an easy walk taking one hour.

From the Mollins beach go up the steps behind the telephone boxes to reach an unsurfaced track. Turn right at the top, then left past the small hotel Los Pinos and turn right again. Go through an old gate at the beginning of a level section, then turn left by an electricity sub-station, then first right by a red arrow. This leads to a cairned footpath across level ground. After dipping into the bed of a little stream this re-joins the main track (which is a continuation of the road running south along the coast from the Mollins beach). This wide track continues past the white Water Board building on the Siller Pass for about 200m and then ends abruptly. From here there are several alternatives but the easiest is to go roughly straight on by a narrow cairned path which leads to the left of the large private house ahead. Pass through some iron gates on the left, where the path becomes a lane between two walls. Turn left at the T-Junction by the Siller gateway and follow the road round until the main road is reached. Turn left and keep straight on the sea-front as in 7(a).

In returning to Cala from the Puerto, the easiest way to find the Siller track is to walk along the Pollensa road to the MIR supermarket just before the petrol station and turn right there.

8. SERRA DEL CAVALL BERNAT

The Cavall Bernat ridge lies between the Cala San Vicente bay and the Boquer valley. Although its maximum height is a modest 375m it has very steep cliffs particularly on the Cala side from where it is both spectacular and beautiful, especially in the late afternoon and evening light when the colour and shadows are constantly changing. From the other side it forms a splendid backdrop to Puerto Pollensa and is seen to advantage when driving along the coastal road from Alcudia. Although this route is not long it includes rough walking and quite difficult scrambling, so is only recommended to experienced walkers who will find it both enjoyable and interesting.

Starting point:	Puerto de Pollensa.
Time:	4hr.20min.
Distance:	8.5km.
Height:	331m., 348m., 291m., 293m., 295m., 375m.
Grade:	A+.
Map:	Cala Sant Vicens 1:25,000 or Pollensa 1:50,000.

Leave Puerto Pollensa by walking along the sea-front as in Walk 7 for the Boquer valley. Continue along the Boquer valley track as far as the second wall crossing the valley; this wall is opposite the obvious col on the ridge to the right of the 'window'. A thin path on the inland side of the wall leads across the valley towards some ruined buildings. From here a way can be found up a shallow gully to the col using the many goat tracks and scree patches between the vegetation. (It is possible to turn right along the ridge and go right out to Troneta, the 340m top at the end, but there are a number of very steep towers which may

Sierra del Cavall Bernat, west top (Walk 8)

involve climbing rather than scrambling.)

From the col, turn left to reach the top of the first tower by quite a steep scramble on sound rock. The steepest part near the top is avoided by a rising traverse out to the left. The hole in the ridge is reached soon after leaving the top of this tower and can be reached quite easily on the Boquer valley side. In fact, any difficulties found along the ridge can be avoided on this side, but it is not always easy to pick out the best way first time. On the rise up to the final top, either continue along the main ridge on the edge of the cliffs, or choose slightly easier walking in a shallow valley on the left. The final top is double and a line of cairns can be followed down from the dip between the two peaks, crossing a wall. Turn right along the second wall to pick up another descending line of cairns at the end of it. When the cairns end, make a slightly rising traverse towards a white building on the Siller Pass road and turn left here to return to Puerto Pollensa.

This walk can equally well be done from Cala San Vicente either by walking over the Siller Pass or using public transport to reach the starting point, and then returning direct to Cala at the end of the walk.

Puerto Pollensa - Col on ridge	1hr.30min.
Col - 375m. top	1hr.30min.
375m top - Coll de Siller	50min.
Coll de Siller - Puerto Pollensa	30min.

The 'window' in the Cavall Bernat Ridge (Walk 8)

Map 6.
Walk 9. La Coma
Walk 10. Puig de S'Aguila
Walk 11. Serra de San Vicens & Mola

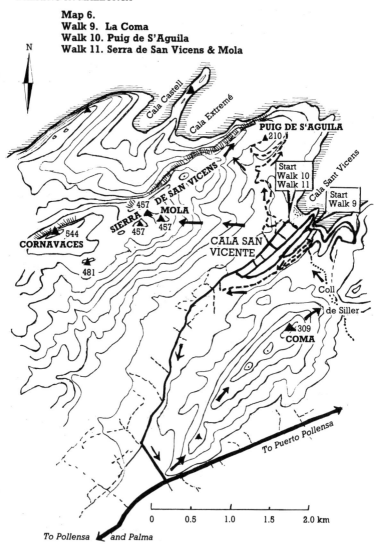

9. LA COMA

A pleasant half-day walk with good views, pathless on the ridge but no route-finding problems. Easily shortened by taking the bus to the road end. (8.45 a.m. weekdays, 10.00 a.m. Sundays).

Starting point:	Cala San Vicente.
Time:	3hr.40min.
Distance:	8.5km.
Height:	309m.
Grade:	C+.
Map:	Pollensa 1:50,000.

From the Mollins beach go up the steps behind the telephone and turn right along the track through the woods. Follow this through a gate and cross the stream to join the main road just outside the village and turn left on this road. At the junction with the Puerto road, go up behind the notice boards and follow the well-defined ridge along over several tops. Sometimes the going is very easy over bare rock ribs, but there is some boulder hopping and some patches of scrub to negotiate.

The last top has a distinctive cairn standing on a circular wall; from here the ridge drops quite steeply towards the Coll de Siller and is rough going in places. At first follow sloping ledges down the rocks, then pick up various hunters' paths leading down in zigzags to the bottom of the crags. The wall across the col can be crossed in several places and the cairned path leading down to Cala San Vicente is then picked up.

Cala San Vicente - road junction	50min.
Road junction - Coma main top	2hr.25min.
Coma main top - Cala San Vicente	1hr.25min.

ASPHODELUS AESTIVUS

10. PUIG DE S'AGUILA

An easy short walk with good views especially in the afternoons when the sun is shining on the Cavall Bernat ridge. Worth taking a torch to look into the rock tunnels leading to old ammunition stores.

Starting point:	Cala San Vicente.
Time:	1hr.45min.
Distance:	4km.
Height:	210m.
Grade:	C.
Map:	Cala Sant Vicens 1:25,000 or Pollensa 1:50,000.

From the Hotel Don Pedro go north on the road along the sea front and follow it round to the left. In about 100m. turn right up a flight of steps between two houses. On the left is a house with a large map of Mallorca on the wall. At the top of the steps fork right to reach the locked gate at the entrance to the quarry road. Access is through a gap in the wall and it is a good track all the way to the quarry where a beautiful white, pink and black rock has been extracted. Further on the track makes a sharp turn left and leads past three tunnels excavated into the rock. The first of these runs straight in for some 40m, then makes a right turn and divides, one part going straight on and the other turning left, then right and right again to meet up with the first part. Above can be seen daylight through the shafts opening on the hilltop. The second tunnel is usually knee deep in water, but from its position must lead to the bottom of the shaft on the top of the Puig de S'Aguila. The third tunnel is very short and has no vertical shaft.

A narrow path continues past the third tunnel and leads up to a col on the west of the Puig de S'Aguila, from where it is only a short distance to the top. The position of the shaft on top is quite obvious, as are the next two shafts reached in a further few minutes. From here a vague path continues down the ridge towards the sea (east), curving round to the right to join the quarry road at the sharp bend. Return along the quarry road, or explore the area between this road and the coast which is pathless but fairly easy walking.

11. SERRA DE SANT VICENT: MOLA

This walk makes a pleasant short day from Cala San Vicente. There are no real paths until the return along the quarry road, but no real difficulties either. All the same it is rough walking and the route finding could become difficult in mist. The views are extensive.

(a) Normal way

Starting point:	Cala San Vicente.
Time:	4hr.15min.
Distance:	6.0km.
Height:	457m.
Grade:	B+.
Map:	Cala Sant Vicens 1:25,000 or Pollensa 1:50,000.

Begin the walk as for Walk 10. From the Hotel Don Pedro take the road along the sea front and follow it round to the left. Immediately after going through the wall by the locked gate, turn left on a rough path. After about 100m leave it and make for the ridge to the left of the end tower. Walk up the first section of the ridge on easy rock to reach a cairn, then cross over a stretch of level ground to the right to reach the off-set continuation of the ridge. At the top of this section there is another cairn. Continue in the same direction, passing the top of a gully which goes down steeply on the right, then making towards a shoulder slightly to the right of the little peak ahead, using goat tracks and solid rock when possible. From this shoulder it is worth the short diversion to the little top on the left from where there is a clear view back down the ridge to Cala San Vicente and the Cavall Bernat ridge.

Ahead is a rock tower, steep at the bottom. Cross the little col and climb up to the left of the tower on easy rock and scree below the steepest rocks. A break in the steep rocks allows a rising traverse right to be made to the top of Mola, one of the three tops that is each marked as 457m. on the map.

Leave the summit by descending to the north and cross the hollow straight ahead to a small rocky top on the far ridge. Turn right (N.E.) along this ridge and descend on good rock, keeping to the edge of the steep ground on the left.

After a short distance (c.500m.) make for a low rocky outcrop in the middle of a slight hollow, following bare rock ribs when possible for the easiest going. Continue in the same general direction, getting closer to the edge of the cliffs again. A short rise is followed by a descent towards a wall, (ignore the red arrow painted on the rock near here which points to the right). A cairn marks the beginning of quite a good narrow path going up towards an indefinite top along the edge of the continuous and impressive cliffs overlooking the sea. Now make for the left top of the two small tops seen ahead and follow on from here to the top of the Puig de S'Aguila. On the top is a hollow and a very deep shaft, and further on a group of 3 shafts with an easy path on each side. Reach the quarry track by going down the ridge towards the sea and keeping slightly to the right. At the end of the track go through the gap in the wall by the locked gate and turn left, then left down the steps to reach the road.

Cala San Vicente - Mola	2h.
Mola - Puig de S'Aguila	1hr.30min.
Puig de S'Aguila - Cala	45min.

(b) Mola: alternative route

This route gains the Serra de San Vicens ridge by a pleasant scramble up an unnamed rock outcrop, reaches the top of Mola from the north-east, then descends the east ridge of Mola back to Cala.

Starting point:	Cala San Vicente.
Time:	4hr.
Distance:	5.5km.
Height:	457m.
Grade:	A+.
Map:	Cala Sant Vicens 1:25,000 or Pollensa 1:50,000.

Leave Cala San Vicente by the quarry road as for Walk 10, Puig de S'Aguila. In about 20 minutes there are two bridges close together. Follow the dry stream bed from the first of these bridges and make for the foot of the right-hand rocky peak at the valley head.

The route goes up by the ridge which forms the right-hand skyline and this can easily be gained if the rock is dry by climbing the bed of the gully direct. If the rocks are wet, it is best to go up diagonally left, then back right to the notch above the steep section. The ridge is mainly good clean rock and there are no difficulties except for a small patch or two of dense vegetation. The tiny flowers of *cyclamen balearicum* can be found here in early April.

The scramble ends at a pleasant little tower. From the top cross two small rocky knolls and keep going in the same direction to a wall. After crossing the wall continue up the vague ridge ahead, choosing bare rock for the easiest walking and as soon as you like walking over to the right to reach the cliff edge. From here there are spectacular views down to the sea and up the Ternelles valley to the Castell del Rei with the steep north face of Cornavaces forming the continuation of the cliffs.

Follow up along the ridge until the ground levels out a little with a rocky top on the left. Go up this by a small but obvious groove to reach one of the three tops of Mola, which have between them a grassy depression. They are all marked as 457m on the map, but the east top appears slightly higher and has a prominent cairn. Cross over to this top either by the rocks on the left or by the depression. To descend, go down at first towards the south-east to avoid some steep ground and find the obvious break in a little escarpment, then down to the right to reach some bare rock ledges. From here go back left and continue in this direction at the foot of the steep rocks to arrive at a small col. Cross this col to the left of the small top ahead and continue down by easy rocks and boulders to another small col. Continue over the next little top and on down the ridge to the steep little tower at the end. Descend to easy ground on the right just before reaching the tower and make for the gate to the quarry road.

Cala San Vicente - Unnamed rocky top	1hr.10min.
Unnamed rocky top - Mola	1hr.20min.
Mola - Cala San Vicente	1hr.30min.

CYCLAMEN BALEARICUM

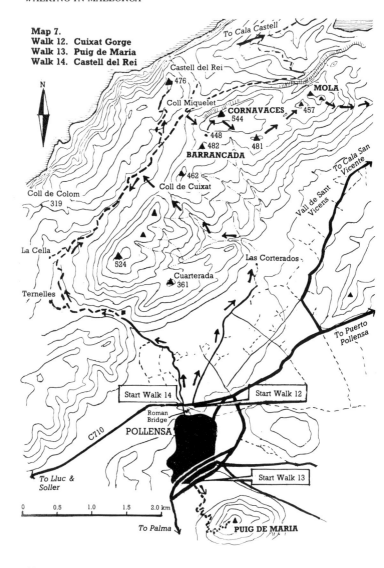

Map 7.
Walk 12. Cuixat Gorge
Walk 13. Puig de Maria
Walk 14. Castell del Rei

N

To Cala Castell

Castell del Rei
476

Coll Miquelet
MOLA
457
CORNAVACES
544
448
482
481
BARRANCADA
462
Coll de Cuixat
Coll de Colom
319
To Cala San Vicente
Vall de Sant Vicens
Las Corterados
La Cella
524
Cuarterada
361
Ternelles
To Puerto Pollensa
Start Walk 14
Start Walk 12
Roman Bridge
C710
POLLENSA
Start Walk 13
To Lluc & Soller

0   0.5   1.0   1.5   2.0 km

To Palma
PUIG DE MARIA

12. CUIXAT GORGE

This walk up the bed of a stream to the Coll de Cuixat is a good introduction to the wild and rough terrain that lies between the Pollensa valley and the northern coast. The route up the gully involves some scrambling up boulders and rocks. There is one quite difficult place but that can be avoided. The return along the Ternelles valley is very easy.

Starting point:	Pollensa.
Time:	4hr.30min.
Distance:	11km.
Height:	362m.
Grade:	A.
Map:	Pollensa 1:25,000 or Pollensa 1:50,000.

From the Pollensa-Lluc road near the Roman Bridge, going towards the east take the first turn left. Keep on this pleasant road through the market gardens in a north-easterly direction, avoiding all turnings until it ends at a house called 'Las Corterados'. The path goes round behind the house to the right so it is advisable to ask for permission first. *(Se puede pasar por aqui?'* with gestures will be enough.) The path keeps to the right of the fields, going through gaps in stone walls and leading to a gate almost at the foot of the gorge but separated from it by an area of very dense trees and shrubs. Turn left after going through the gate then through whatever gaps can be found, until it is possible to reach a wall at the foot of the rocks guarding the entrance to the gorge on the left.

Once over the wall a good path can be picked up and followed upwards into a small cwm. A scramble up some steep rocks on the left at the head of this leads to a small ledge from where it is easy to drop down into a hidden valley. Turn left here and follow the stream bed up to a junction, where the right branch should be taken and followed until a rather steep little chimney is encountered. This is the only difficult bit and it can be avoided by going out to the left and then back right into the bed of the stream. At the next junction, again take the right hand branch and continue up until a little head wall is reached. Easy climbing up this wall leads to a gently sloping valley which leads in ten minutes to the Coll de Cuixat, from where there are excellent views of the Castell del Rei and the Puig Gros de Ternelles. (Walk 14 and 15).

Go down from the col, steeply at first and then across the valley on a forest track to reach the Ternelles valley road. Turn left here and follow the road back to Pollensa. (Drinking water is available from a tapped fountain on the left of the track, just before the second locked gate and after about 1hr. of walking down the valley.)

Pollensa - foot of gorge	30min.
Foot of gorge - Coll de Cuixat	2hr.25min.
Coll de Cuixat - Pollensa	1hr.35min.

13. PUIG DE MARIA

An easy attractive walk with excellent views, very near Pollensa so easily accessible by public transport. There is a sanctuary on top where accommodation is available at a small charge. There are also kitchens and a large refectory, for use of which a donation is requested. Soft drinks, sandwiches and excellent coffee are on sale at a small kiosk inside the entrance hall. There has been a chapel on the site since 1348, and in 1362 the establishment was being run by three women, who were the first female hermits in the history of the Baleares. Many local people go up there on Sundays and on Easter Monday almost the entire population of Pollensa is there, either in the refectory or the outside picnic area.

Starting point:	Pollensa.
Time:	1hr.30min.
Distance:	3.5km.
Height:	270m.
Grade:	C.
Map:	Pollensa 1:25,000 or Pollensa 1:50,000.

From the petrol station in Pollensa, follow the signposted road 'Puig de Maria' across the main Palma road and up the narrow winding lane. Turn sharp right at the first bend, then left past several terraced gardens and fields. At first the road is surfaced, but very narrow, and there is scarcely any parking space at the road end. From the end of the road a narrow path leads in fifteen minutes to the walled terrace at the side of the chapel.

From Puig de Maria (Walk 13)

14. CASTELL DEL REI

The situation of the ruined Castell del Rei, overlooking the sea from the edge of very steep cliffs is extremely impressive. It was an important stronghold for the Arabs, but was taken by Jaime I c.1230 by offering good terms to the defenders. Later it was besieged by Aragonese invaders in 1285 and again in 1343, but eventually had to surrender. The walk to the castle today is very easy but quite long; the road to it is a private one running through the wooded Ternelles valley, a good place for birds. Black vultures are sometimes seen near the castle itself.

(a). Normal way by Ternelles

Starting point:	Crossroads on C710 near Roman Bridge, Pollensa.
Time:	4hr.15min.
Distance:	13km.
Height:	476m.
Grade:	C.
Map:	Pollensa 1:50,000.

The narrow road to Ternelles begins just outside Pollensa at a signposted crossroads on the Lluc road C710, just past the Roman Bridge.

69

It is possible to park in the town near here, by turning into Pollensa at the crossroads and taking the first left. (To walk here from the bus station, turn left and go up through the main square (Plaza Mayor), up to the right of the church, turn right at the end, then right into a small square with a fountain, left here, then right into the Calle de la Huerta. Fork right at the end to reach the crossroads.)

On the way to Ternelles the road goes through a very attractive area of market gardens with almond orchards and orange trees. As it enters the 'Narrows' the remains of a Roman aqueduct may be seen. Beyond the locked gates at the entrance to the Ternelles property (there is a pedestrian access gate) the road becomes unsurfaced. 100m after passing a large house drinking water may be obtained from a brass tap on the right of the track. This is spring water which local people come to collect in large plastic water bottles.

Another access gate is provided at the second locked gates, after which the track begins to rise up towards the Coll Miquelet. Shortly after crossing a cattle grid the track divides into two; take the right fork which is signposted 'Castell del Rei' and continue uphill until the trees thin out and the castle can be seen in the distance. The left fork that leads to the castle is not very obvious as the track has been damaged by floods. It will be found 100m beyond the start of a fenced area on the right. This track ends at a flat area just below the castle, and a narrow path leads up to the gateway arch which is the entrance to the ruins. These cover an extensive area and it is worth spending some time here.

Return by the same way, or follow the Castell del Rei ridge south west to the Coll de Colom and pick up the path which leads back to the Ternelles valley by Sa Cella (see Walk 18). Allow an extra 20min. for this. *(Benigne Palos, p.152)*

Pollensa - Castell del Rei	2hr.15min.
Castell del Rei - Pollensa	2hr.

(b). Castell del Rei and Cornavaces

This walk ends at a different place from the starting point. It is particularly suited to those based at Cala San Vicente where the walk ends: there is, however, a bus from Cala to Pollensa at 18.45 for those who are not. There is also the option of climbing Cornavaces and returning by the Ternelles valley to Pollensa.

Castell del Rei (Walk 14)

Starting point:	Pollensa crossroads near Roman Bridge.
Time:	6hr.30min.
Distance:	12km.
Height:	476m, 544m, 457m.
Grade:	A.
Map:	Pollensa 1:50,000 or Pollensa 1:25,000 and Cala Sant Vicens 1:25,000.

After visiting the Castell del Rei as in Walk 14(a), return to the main valley track and turn left towards the coast. As soon as the cultivated fields are passed, turn right along a wall and at the corner turn right along another wall until an easy way to strike up to the col between Cornavaces and Barrancada can be found. Turn left at the col and follow the ridge up to the top, keeping near the cliffs for some striking views of the steep north east face of Cornavaces. From the top it is an easy walk across a dip and up to the top of the 481m top of the Serra de San Vicens ridge. Follow this ridge along to Mola, a triple top of 457m and then go down the east ridge to Cala San Vicente as in Walk 11(b).

Pollensa - Castell del Rei	2hr.15min.
Castell del Rei - Cornavaces	1hr.45min.
Cornavaces - Mola	1hr.
Mola - Cala San Vicente	1hr.30min.

15. PUIG GROS DE TERNELLES

This is a strenuous walk, much of it over rough and trackless ground and only recommended for experienced walkers well used to route finding. There are some very fine situations overlooking the sea and there is a fair chance of seeing black vultures.

Starting point:	The Roman Bridge, Pollensa.
Time:	7hr.40min.
Distance:	15km.
Height:	838m.
Grade:	A+.
Map:	Pollensa 1:50,000.

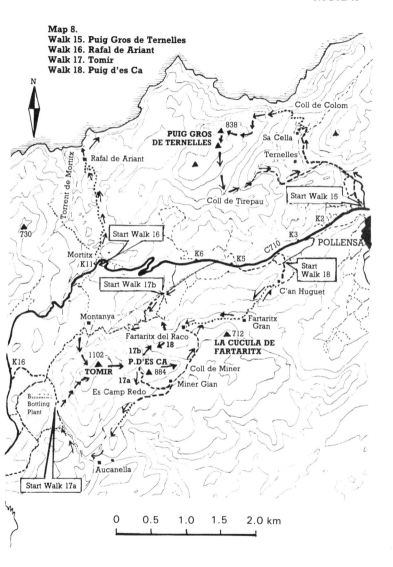

Map 8.
Walk 15. Puig Gros de Ternelles
Walk 16. Rafal de Ariant
Walk 17. Tomir
Walk 18. Puig d'es Ca

N

Coll de Colom

838

**PUIG GROS
DE TERNELLES**

Sa Cella

Rafal de Ariant

Ternelles

Torrent de Mortitx

Coll de Tirepau

Start Walk 15

730

K2

Start Walk 16

K3

K6   K5

C710

POLLENSA

Mortitx
K11

Start Walk 17b

Start
Walk 18

C'an Huguet

Montanya

Fartaritx
Gran

Fartaritx del Raco

712

17b   18

**LA CUCULA DE
FARTARITX**

K16

1102

P.D'ES CA

TOMIR   884

Coll de Miner

17a

Miner Gian

Es Camp Redo

Binnuac
Bottling
Plant

Aucanella

Start Walk 17a

0   0.5   1.0   1.5   2.0 km

Leave Pollensa by the Roman Bridge. If it is your first visit to the town and you get lost in the maze of narrow streets, ask anyone for *'El Puenta Romana'*. By car, take the Lluc road and turn into Pollensa just above the Roman Bridge, opposite the Ternelles road and find a parking place nearby.

Follow the Ternelles road as for the Castell del Rei (Walk 14). After the first cattle grid, take the left fork. (The right fork is signposted Castell del Rei.) After crossing a little bridge and about 5 minutes further on a path on the right will be seen, marked by a red arrow painted on a rock. This goes up at the side of a stream bed, yellow arrows now marking the way, first left and then right to cross an old aqueduct where a track leading up to the right will be found. After a sudden increase in gradient this track narrows and levels out before rising again towards the Coll de Colom. Watch out for a right turn where a painted sign on a rock is almost obscured by vegetation. The path, now very narrow, becomes confused with animal tracks, but it is easy enough to make for the col which is the obvious cleft on the left of a rocky outcrop. Here there is a sudden and dramatic view of the coast and the next part of the route, with a look back to the wooded Ternelles valley with its cultivated fields surrounded by woods.

The way ahead at first sight looks impracticable, but looking down towards the sea a narrow path will be observed to contour the bottom of the crags and disappear round the corner. Follow this and it will be found to contour along the sloping shelf which lies between the crags and the steep ground dropping to the sea. After about 15-20 minutes this path turns left and goes into a wide gully leading steeply upwards through prickly scrub to a flat rocky outcrop. After this it is hard work continuing up a rather unstable scree slope until you can make your way out to the right, to a patch of level ground known as the Coll de la Reteta. From here the top of the Puig Gros can be seen ahead, but the way to get there is a little devious. First turn slightly left, crossing below some shrubs and over rock to a small plain, the 'Pla de les Mates Velles'. Make for a cairn on the far side of this and pick up a good path leading up a narrow valley on the right, giving access to a large amphitheatre in the centre of which is a steep rock wall. Go over well to the right of this, looking out for a stone wall by a patch of burnt ground with a cairn. From here a rough path up a gully leads to the summit ridge which is followed up to the top, on which is a cairn and a metal plaque inscribed *'Grup Excursionista d'Inca'*. There are extensive views, especially good over the north east of the island.

The way down lies to the south (170°), keeping the rocky tooth 'El Mola' on the right. This part of the walk is very rough going indeed, over very broken ground, and it is nowhere easy to pick the best way. It is necessary to reach the Coll de Tirapau (475m) which is marked on the map, and near here some sticks with the 'private hunting' signs give an indication of the way. From the col, turn left (north east) down the valley, still rough going until the forest track can be reached. From here follow the main track down to join the Ternelles valley track by some stepping stones over the stream.

Pollensa - Coll de Colom	1hr.30min.
Coll de Colom - Puig Gros de Ternelles	2hr.40min.
Puig Gros - Coll de Tirapau	1hr.30min.
Coll de Tirapau - Pollensa	2hr.

16. RAFAL DE ARIANT

The area between the Puig Roig and the Puig Gros de Ternelles is without doubt the roughest and wildest area of the Sierra de Tramuntana. There are incredible rock formations and the scenery is most impressive all the way down to the coast where huge caves can be seen in the cliffs. The abandoned house Rafal de Ariant is in a wonderful situation on a flat shelf about 160m above the sea.

Starting point:	Mortaitx gates, K10.9 on C710
Time:	4hr. (to Rafal de Ariant and return)
Distance:	8km.
Height:	220m. (descent)
Grade:	B+.
Map:	Pollensa 1:50,000.

A car can be left near the Mortaitx gates at K10.9. Go through two gates, pass the tennis court, then through another gate to the left of a stone building and continue between peach orchards to another gate. After passing a fig tree the path rises slightly to yet another gate. At a prominent and colourful marker stone take the left fork and follow the path down through woodland. There are red paint marks here but they are not always easy to see. Go through a gate at the junction of two stone walls and follow the path through this wild and rocky area. Cairns and red paint marks make this reasonably easy, but look out for two places where the path makes a sudden right turn. After going

Rafal de Ariant (Walk 16)

through a gap in a stone wall the path swings left and then descends a cliff in tight zigzags to the plain behind Rafal de Ariant.

From the house it is a further ten minutes or so to the edge of the cliffs and a view of an impressive cave high up on the right. Another narrow path leads from the house over the low Coll de la Caleta and then descends towards the coast. This becomes steep and loose, but it is worth the effort for the views of the coast at the Caleta de Ariant. The Cova de Ses Bruixes is high up in the steep hillside on the left and is most easily seen by crossing over to the right from a very large boulder encountered on the path about twenty minutes walk from the house. Allow an extra fifty minutes at least for this extension of the walk.

Return to Mortaitx by the same path as used on the way out.

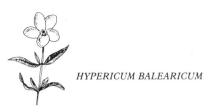

HYPERICUM BALEARICUM

17. PUIG TOMIR

(a). From Binifaldo, return by Aucanella

Tomir is as well-known and as popular as Massanella, owing to its commanding position at the head of the Pollensa valley and its accessibility. It can be reached in 1hr.30min. from the road end at Binifaldo by a good path and is known to be one of the places where black vultures may be sighted. For these reasons it is a mountain where other walkers are likely to be met. The return route on this walk however is by little used paths where other people are seldom encountered. The views from the top are extensive, and a point of interest is the deep snow-pit near the summit.

Starting point:	Binifaldo Bottling plant.
Time:	5hr.
Distance:	7km.
Height:	1,102m.
Grade:	A.
Map:	Pollensa 1:50,000 and Inca 1:50,000 or Son March 1:25,000 and Selva 1:25,000.

To reach Binifaldo turn left at K17.4 on the Pollensa-Lluc road, through a gateway with a *'Ministerio de Agricultura'* sign. Take the left fork when two green gates are reached and continue until the road ends at the bottling plant, where there is a parking place.

The route starts between the gate to the plant and the forest fence. Follow the boundary fence until a painted arrow marks a sharp right turn and the path begins to wind up through the trees. After leaving the woods there is a level section and then a rising traverse above a scree. After crossing a second and wider scree the path rises steeply to a little col, on the other side of which it continues to rise steeply, keeping close against the base of the rocks on the right. In the main the path is a good one with rock steps built up in the steeper places. It leads in a further fifteen minutes from the col to a little rock wall about 4m high. This is easily surmounted by a groove sloping up diagonally from right to left and well-supplied with hand and footholds.

Above the wall the path continues upwards in a shallow valley which leads directly to the summit ridge. However, it is easier, because not so loose and stony, to leave this valley in a few minutes by a cairned path on the right, only turning left towards the head of the valley when another line of cairns is reached. On arriving at a small col between two tops of the main ridge, turn left and follow the cairns up gently rising ground to the summit.

From the top go down east to reach the *casa de ñieve* in ten minutes, then continue down towards the Coll d'es Puig d'es Ca. In places the remains of the old track used by the *navaters* can be picked out. Aim slightly to the right of the col at first to avoid some steep ground, then towards the centre where a land-rover track will be found. Turn right along this and follow it down past a small hollow on the right. When another track is met turn right again to reach a flat plain known as the Camp Redo. From the turning circle at the end of the track a little path leads to a gap in the boundary wall and on through a narrow valley which skirts the south-east slopes of Tomir.

There are occasional cairns on this path which leads to the ruined house Aucanella, then turns west across a flat area. The path now leads up to the Coll des Pedregaret and is easy to follow. After crossing the stream bed it rises high on the left side of the valley where it is well-marked by cairns. Higher up it goes into the forest, the Bosc Gran (or big wood), then crosses the stream to join a cart-track. This rises to reach the col by the forest gate at Binifaldo.

Binifaldo - Tomir	1hr.30min.
Tomir - Coll d'es Puig d'es Ca	45min.
Coll - Camp Redo	30min.
Camp Redo - Aucanella	1hr.
Aucanella - Binifaldo	1hr.15min.

(b). From Pollensa Valley

This alternative way up Tomir is a long and strenuous one involving a scramble up one of the northern ridges and a pathless descent. It is a very satisfying way up because Tomir dominates the Pollensa valley and it is an interesting route making use of a now little-used old road with views of the steep northern slopes of the mountain. The descent goes past one of the most fascinating of all the snow-houses on the island, although this can also be seen on Walk 18.

This route is for experienced walkers only.

Starting point:	Pollensa-Binifaldo road.
Time:	7hr.
Distance:	11km.
Height:	1,107m.
Grade:	A+.
Map:	Pollensa 1:50,000.

Turn left from the Pollensa-Lluc road C710 at K5.5, signposted 'Las Creus'. A place can be found to leave a car at the side of this road somewhere near the signpost on the left to 'Es Pujol'. Walk up the valley along the old road towards Tomir. At Ca'n Melsion the road turns sharp left, then bends right, after which there is an unlocked gate across the road. Soon the road swings sharp right; the track on the left here is the return route for this walk. The gravel surface now ends, just by the locked gate to Ca'n Cunat. The old road continues to be well defined but so many trees were brought down by the very heavy and unusual snow in January 1985 that progress is quite slow. After rising through the forest in a series of hairpins the road crosses a plateau of cultivated ground before reaching the edge of the woods below the northern cliffs of Tomir. Ignore a new track on the right not shown on the map and continue along the old road which crosses a stream near the farm 'Montanya'. Take the left turn after this and after several bends look out for an old cairn on the left, just below a *sitja*. There is no real path here and it is a question of finding a way up through the trees to the open ground of the ridge above. This ridge is an obvious one bounded on the left by a deeply cut gully and forming a watershed between the Torrent Son March of the Pollensa valley and the Torrent de Mortitx further west. The line of the ridge is easy to follow, with any difficulties being avoided on the right. There are no real difficulties, although some loose rock may be met with in the upper part, shortly before the summit ridge is reached. The summit ridge is then followed left along the edge of the crags, or slightly to the right of it where cairns show the easiest walking.

From the top, descend to the Coll d'es Puig d'es Ca passing a snow pit and making use of the remains of an old path. From the Coll, turn left and cross the fence by a cairn, where a path will be found leading down (north) to the *casa de la neu.*

From here the old path has almost completely disappeared, but the going is fairly easy in a north-easterly direction towards the farm 'Fartaritx del Raco'. Before reaching the farm go through a gap in a wall on the left on the other side of which an old path can be found. This traverses to the west and crosses a stream at the head of a steep valley, then leads down into the valley before becoming lost above the forest. After entering the forest the way is a little confused, but keep near the stream to avoid some steep ground and then pick up the old track which leads past an old farm and eventually rejoins the route of ascent near Ca'n Cunat.

Pollensa valley, 'El Pujol' sign - Foot of ridge	2hr.15min.
Foot of ridge - Tomir summit	2hr.
Tomir - Coll d'es Puig de Ca	45min.
Coll - 'El Pujol' sign	2hr.

18. PUIG D'ES CA

The Puig d'es Ca is somewhat dwarfed by Tomir and is not so spectacular as the Cuculla del Fartaritx, the third of the three mountains which dominate the Pollensa valley. However, it provides an interesting walk by an excellent path which leads up through woods to the high pastures on the sloping shelf overlooking this valley. The *casa de la neu* seen on Walk 21(b) is also a feature of the walk.

Starting point:	Ca'n Huguet.
Time:	5hr.45min.
Distance:	12.0km.
Height:	885m.
Grade:	A.
Map:	Pollensa 1:50,000.

Turn left off the Pollensa-Lluc road at K2.7, cross the bridge and turn right. It is possible to find places to leave a small car along this lane which leads to Ca'n Huguet. This is a newish house with a swimming pool and the track passes in front of it, then doubles back and goes up behind it to an older, possibly abandoned, house. Go up the steps in front of this old house, pass a well and go through a gate into a wood where there are often pigs feeding on the acorns of the evergreen oaks. The path is easy to follow up through these woods. Turn left along a forest road which is met on the far side of a stone wall. This track leads to a gate and a mule track which gives access to the *finca* at the eastern end of the upper plateau, Fartaritx Gran. (This lies at 464m and is wrongly labelled Ca'n Huguet on the map.)

Just before Fartaritx Gran the path crosses a stream and turns right alongside a wall, going through two gates. Continuing in the same direction, go through another gate just before the ruined house Fartaritx d'en Vila. Turn left up the steps half hidden among the trees and go between the old buildings. Then turn right and continue along the track in the same direction as before. There is a locked gate to surmount at a boundary fence, after which it is better to skirt round to

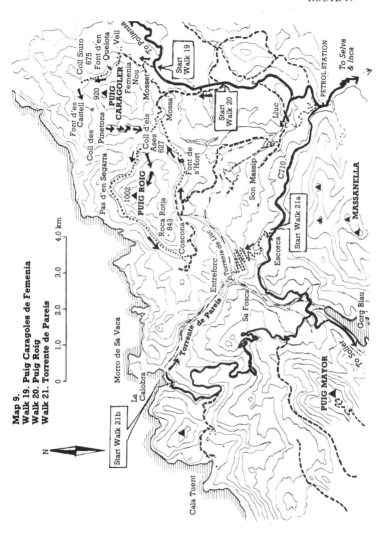

Map 9.
Walk 19. Puig Caragoles de Femenia
Walk 20. Puig Roig
Walk 21. Torrente de Pareis

the north of the last *finca*, Fartaritx del Raco, as at the present time walkers do not appear to be welcome here. Once this is passed, make towards the Coll d'es Puig de Ca, using what traces of the old path remain. (This part of the walk is used as a descent in Walk 17(b). The upper part above the old snowhouse is quite steep but the path becomes more evident. Go through the hole in the fence to reach the col, where a wide track leading south commences.

Follow this track to the boundary wall and then turn left into a shallow gully, making for a low crag at the top. There is an easy way up a sloping ledge and the west top is reached after a further few minutes. Double back to continue over the main top and along the ridge down to the Coll de Miner, crossing the wall near the crag as there is a high locked gate on the col itself. Follow the new track, not on the map, which leads to Fartaritx del Raco, but leave it where it bends left. Cut across the corner to reach the track leading back to the ruined house and return by the good path used on the ascent.

To find the way down, turn sharp left after passing through a self-closing gate, just before reaching the farm Fartaritx Gran.

Ca'n Huguet - Fartaritx Gran	1hr.15min.
Fartaritx Gran - Coll d'es Puig de Ca	1hr.30min.
Coll d'es Puig de Ca - Puig d'es Ca	45min.
Puig d'es Ca - Coll Miner	30min.
Coll Miner - Ca'n Huguet	1hr.45min.

19. A CIRCUIT OF THE PUIG CARAGOLER DE FEMENIA

This massif lies between the Puig Roig and the Puig Gros de Ternelles,north of the Lluc-Pollensa road. Although the walk is neither long nor difficult it is partly pathless and some route-finding experience is desirable. It is not recommended in mist. The scenery is wild and attractive and it is rare to meet other people.

Starting point:	K14.2, Lluc-Pollensa road.
Time:	3hr.50min.
Distance:	10.0km.
Height:	675m, c.685m, 627m.
Grade:	B + .
Map:	Pollensa 1:50,000.

The route begins at the entrance to Femenia Nou on the Lluc-Pollensa road. Parking for one car may be found about 200m further on towards Lluc and there are other spaces near the Mossa gates at

K14.4. The main gate is locked, but there is an access stile on the left. In a short distance take a left fork and go through the gate behind Femenia Nou, continuing to Femenia Vell where the track appears to end. The continuation of the track doubles back exactly by the house and leads through the pinewoods on to the east side of Puig Caragoler. This wide track ends at a spring, the Font d'en Quelota, where water gushes out of the rock into a stone trough which is roofed over and gated. A glass tumbler will be found inside. From the fountain a rather narrow and overgrown path leads on to the Coll Ciuró (or Siuró), at first descending slightly and then rising below the cliffs of Caragoler. From the Coll Ciuró there is at first no path. Cross the small flat plain just over the col and make for the top of the low line of rocks between this plain and another one just below. Aim to keep above a windswept tree and contour along at this level, rising slightly to cross through a low wall and then making for a ruined building. From here follow a narrow sheep track to reach a large cairn, then descend gradually to some old terraces. There are traces of old paths and some small cairns along here leading past another spring, the Font d'en Castell, which is roofed. This can be picked out from a distance by the green damp area below it surrounded by a wall. From here descend slightly left then ascend right to arrive at the Coll d'es Pinetons where there is a marker cairn. From a distance this looks like an enormous structure, but turns out to be a tiny heap of stones on a large pointed rock.

From the Coll d'es Pinetons traverse left, descending very slightly at first then more steeply down a narrow gully. The path twists and turns into a wider valley where it becomes more difficult to follow, but it does continue in the general direction of the Coll d'els Ases. Soon a shallow gully rises to the left and leads to the zigzags of an old path rising to the col. These are not easy to follow continuously but the going is fairly good everywhere. Once on the col, the excellent path descending to Mossa is picked up. From Mossa, follow the track towards the C710, in a few minutes turning left at an acute angle to go behind Mosset to join the Femenia Neu track, turning right along this to return to the starting point.

K14.2 - Font d'en Quelota	30min.
Font - Coll Siuró	30min.
Coll Siuró - Coll d'es Pinetons	50min.
Coll d'es Pinetons - Coll d'els Ases	1hr.
Coll d'es Ases - K.14.2	1hr.

Tomir from Fartaritx del Raco (Walk 19)

20. PUIG ROIG

The Puig Roig, or Red Peak, is a most attractive mountain almost entirely encircled by steep red cliffs. It looks especially striking when seen from the Soller-Lluc road in the evening light and it is always worth stopping at the small mirador between Escorca and the Gorg Blau if returning this way from some other excursion. The circular walk described (20a) is almost entirely on an excellent corniche path, a former smugglers' route with some unsurpassed views of the coast. The path on the south east side is more difficult to follow, but interesting. The ascent (20b) can be made most easily from the Coll d'els Ases, but a more interesting way is to follow the ridge up from near Coscona to the Roca Rotja and then descend to the Coll d'els Ases.

(a). Circuit of the Puig Roig

Starting point:	Mossa gates on C710, K15.
Time:	5hr.30min.
Distance:	14km.
Height:	Highest point (Pas d'en Segarra) c.700m.
Grade:	B+.
Map:	Pollensa 1:50,000.

84

A small car may be parked just opposite the Mossa gates. Follow the track to the *finca*, a large sheep-farm, and go through the gate at the far side of the house. Cross the clearing straight ahead to find the beginning of the excellent path that leads up to the Coll d'els Ases. This path slopes obliquely up the side of a very steep cliff and at one time had protective handrails, now disappeared. From the pass follow the path around the northern slopes towards the coast; (there are a number of good bivvy sites here under overhanging rocks).

At the most northerly point the path turns a corner (the Pas d'en Segarra), then runs south west, contouring below the cliffs with excellent views of the old Torre de Lluc and the spectacular Morro de Sa Vaca. Further south there is a sudden view of the Puig Mayor. After crossing a stile by a sheep-fold the ruined barracks of the customs officials comes into sight below. Go through a gap in the wall above the barracks. The path then traverses to join the track from the customs house near the old houses of Coscona, built under the overhanging rocks. (Alternatively, follow the wall down to the ruined building and pick up the track there, or make towards a water-tank behind which there is a spring.)

Two minutes or so after passing Coscona and just before the track bends to the left, look out for a narrow path beginning by a double-trunked olive tree growing at the edge of the road. (Ignore the first narrow path a few metres before this.) This excellent path then contours along the southern slopes of the Puig Roig and at first is very easy to follow, with cairns and red paint marks in one or two places where it has been invaded by vegetation. When the pinewood is reached, keep on the terrace above the fig-tree, then climb up to the next terrace by a red paint mark. The path then levels out again until it reaches a clearing at the further edge of the woods. Here a large boulder with three red paint marks indicates the place where a short descent is made to a terrace. Turn left here and go through the opening in the wall, following the path along old olive terraces until a large circular platform, an old threshing-floor, is reached.

From here the path rises slightly to go above an enclosure with an old building. Behind this is a spring hidden by brambles in an underground tunnel. The water here is heard rather than seen, and in dry weather may not be noticed. The path next crosses a stream bed before dropping down by some old terraces, contouring along one of these below a wall with a fence on top. Paint marks and cairns are then followed along a rather overgrown section, then down a short slope of more open ground to a gate leading into a wood of evergreen oaks.

The path now keeps within the wood all the way to Mossa, never going far from the boundary wall. After a gate with a triple fastening is reached (easier to climb by one of the gateposts), the path becomes very vague, especially near the *finca* where the ground has been churned up by animals. Keep within sight of the boundary wall to arrive at a small clearing behind the buildings.

Mossa gates - Mossa	30min.
Mossa - Coll d'els Ases	25min.
Coll d'els Ases - Pas d'en Segarra	55min.
Pas d'en Segarra - Coscona	1hr.30min.
Coscona - Threshing floor	1hr.
Threshing floor - Mossa	55min.
Mossa - Mossa gate	30min.

(b). Ascent of Puig Roig

Although the Puig Roig is the lowest of the 1,000m summits, the traverse from south to north over a secondary top at 843m gives a long walk over very rough ground. There are no paths on the mountain, very few cairns, and some scrambling is involved, so this walk is only recommended to those with a fair amount of experience in route finding on difficult terrain.

Starting point:	Mossa gate, K15.8 on C710.
Time:	7hr.
Distance:	15km.
Height:	1,002m.
Grade:	A+.
Map:	Pollensa 1:50,000 or Vall Son March 1:25,000.

From K15.8 follow the main track to the large *finca* of Mossa as in Walk 20(a). Go through the gate at the side of the buildings and then bear left into the woods. Turn left again and descend towards the wall, across ground broken up by animals, and continue walking through the woods fairly near the wall. After about fifteen minutes climb over a cross wall by a gate well fastened up with twisted wires. The path then becomes more obvious and there are some cairns and red paint marks, leading to a gate at the end of the wood. Go through here and turn right, following more paint marks and cairns up through several old terraces, rather overgrown in places. The path then turns a corner on a terrace below a wall with a fence on top, and gives a sudden view of the Puig Mayor. At the end of this terrace a red spot shows the way up a collapsed wall and along another terrace to cross a stream-bed. From here the path goes through a thicket of narrow-leaved cistus, just behind another wall with fence. At the end of this there is a spring hidden by brambles, which will be heard rather than seen and may not be noticed in dry weather. At this point avoid the more obvious path going straight on but bear slightly left to reach a prominent circular platform - an old threshing floor. From here the path continues through some broad terraces to a gateway. A few metres beyond the gate, go up fairly steeply into the pinewood. By a large boulder with red paint marks the path levels out and leads through to the far side of the wood. There is a gap in the fence here and the path continues in a slightly rising traverse across the open hillside. In places it is overgrown but quite easy to follow. Finally it joins the track that goes from Lluc to Coscona by a distinctive olive tree with a double trunk at the side of the road. Turn right and after passing the houses of Coscona take a narrow path on the right to reach a gap in the wall above the abandoned customs barracks.

Turn right by the side of the wall to reach a gate at the foot of the crags. The next part is easy scrambling, picking out the best way by various broad cracks and ledges to reach the foot of some steep rocks which are the true end of the ridge. A series of sloping slabs can then be followed up to reach a low rock wall, easily climbed in two or three places. From this point it is then a pleasant walk along the ridge to the first top. A short descent is then made to the col at 788m, after which the terrain becomes much rougher. It is fairly slow going picking out the best way up the rather indefinite ridge from here to the Puig Roig.

To descend, follow the ridge back to the minor col between the main top and the 959m top, then swing south east to join a ridge running east. This ridge is more well-defined than appears on the map. Follow it until a shallow valley can be seen on each side of the ridge and pick out a short but steep way down into the left-hand valley (north). Continue down this sloping valley to the top of a broad gully with a distinctive rocky hump on the right. Some cairns show the way here. At the bottom of the gully turn left along the foot of some steep rocks until a cairn shows the way down left into another valley. Follow this down bearing first left then right to reach the 'smugglers' path about 50m to the left of a prominent tree. Turn right to reach the Coll d'els Ases and follow the path down to Mossa.

K15.8 - Mossa	30min.
Mossa - Threshing floor	45min.
Threshing floor - gap in wall	1hr.15min.
Wall - first top	1hr.
First top - Puig Roig	1hr.
Puig Roig - Col d'els Ases	1hr.40min.
Col d'els Ases - Mossa	20min.
Mossa - K15.8	30min.

21. TORRENTE DE PAREIS

This walk is one of the most popular on the island, going through a narrow gorge between limestone cliffs 300-400m high. The scenery is wild and spectacular and the stream disgorges into the sea at a lovely bay with clear turquoise and deep blue waters between rocky headlands. However, it is not a walk for the inexperienced or the unfit. In fact, it is more of a scramble that involves some rock-climbing of the moderate-difficult category, the rocks can be wet and slippery and there may be quite deep pools of water to be waded through. The difficult places are only short however, and there is little exposure, so that anyone used to rough scrambling can tackle the walk with confidence, especially if the advice given here is followed and the gorge explored from either the top or the bottom and a return made the same way.

It is usually advised that the only time to do the walk is in the summer and it is certainly easier then when there will be scarcely any water in the pools and the rocks will be completely dry. However, most people coming to Mallorca for a walking holiday will be avoiding the hottest summer months and many well choose the winter months from November until April. In this case it is essential to choose a day when there has been a longish period without rain, or there can be so much water in the pools that the gorge is impassable.

Having said all that, a visit to the gorge is thoroughly recommended and it is well worth devoting two days to it rather than trying to do a through-trip. This in any case involves either doing the double walk which is extremely strenuous, or making complicated transport arrangements for return to your starting point.

(a). Escorca to the Entreforc and return

The Entreforc is the place where the two streams, Lluc and La Fosca meet and continue as the Torrente de Pareis (twin streams) to the sea.

This walk is much the easiest part of the gorge and there is ample time in the day to include a diversion to the entrance to the cave system of La Fosca and to continue beyond the Entreforc as far as the first large boulders which make the going a lot more difficult.

Starting point:	Restaurante de Escorca.
Time:	3-4hrs.
Distance:	c.6km.
Height:	Descent from 650m to 180m (and return).
Grade:	B.
Map:	Pollensa 1:50,000 and Inca 1:50,000.

From the car park opposite the Restaurante Escorca, go to the right of the small 13th century church of Sant Pere and immediately turn up some steps on the left by an old olive tree. At the top of the steps turn right along the path towards the farm to arrive at two gates. Turn through the left one and in a minute or two turn left again at a new wooden signpost, just past a very large and incongruous dustbin. Follow the path down near the edge of a wood, climbing over a stile by a small iron gate and continuing in the same direction until an old olive tree with a black circle painted on it indicates a sharp left turn. The path then makes its way down a small cliff, turning first left then right, after which it is easy to follow right down to the gorge in a series of bends. About 20m after passing a fig tree a small path leads off right between clumps of coarse grass and goes down into the bed of the Lluc stream. Once in the stream bed turn left and look out for another small path on the left which avoids some boulders. Continue to the Entreforc with no difficulties. At the Entreforc is a stone marked as a cross-roads and pointing the way to Lluc, to La Calobra, to Sa Fosca and *'Millor no eneri'*. This latter points to the vertical rock wall and means 'better not go' in Mallorquin.

The easiest way to reach the entrance to La Fosca is by keeping near the rock wall on the left. It is worth going in a few metres until the walls meet overhead and the increasing darkness make it advisable to return to daylight and continue the walk. (Caving experience and equipment are needed to explore any further here.)

Return to the Entreforc and look out for a small path on the right, indicated by red paint marks, which leads down the gorge towards La Calobra and avoids some large boulders. In about 20 minutes the top of some enormous blocks will be reached and it is recommended that a return is made from this point.

(b) Sa Calobra to Entreforc and return

All the difficulties of the gorge are in this section and it should be attempted, as said before, either in summer or after a dry period. Sometimes bad flooding can occur at the mouth of the gorge, either because of higher tides in spring and autumn combined with rain, or by flash floods after storms. Should you be unfortunate enough to be caught in the gorge when something of the sort happens, it may be useful to know that there is an 'escape route' over the rocks on the south side of the tunnel. It begins from the slopes of the amphitheatre quite near the tunnel and if you look back towards the tunnel on your way up the gorge you will see some old steps leading up into a steep narrow gully to a col. The steps have disappeared in places, but there are no difficulties. Once on the col, keep to the left gully on the other side; it leads down to the path near the car park.

Starting point:	Sa Calobra, tunnel exit.
Time:	5-6 hours.
Distance:	7km.
Height:	180m.
Grade:	A+.
Map:	Inca 1:50,000.

N.B. All 'lefts' and 'rights' in the following description are for anyone looking *up* the gorge.

Go through the tunnel from the path at the end of the car park into the wide amphitheatre hidden behind the rocks. (If the conditions are right for the walk there should only be a trickle of water in the stream bed that runs across the flat plain here to disappear into the small shingle beach.) Sa Calobra is a very popular place and if you are unlucky there may be coach loads of people here, but of the few who set off towards the gorge, most return after 10 minutes when they come to a place where a few easy boulders have to be surmounted on the left. After this there is an easy section where pools can be avoided without much trouble, then a stretch of around 50m. where small stones give easy walking up to some large but easy blocks spanning the gorge. This is followed by more boulders and another flat stony section which leads to the narrows and the first little difficulty. This is a very large boulder with a pool at the bottom. The way goes up by the wall on the right, by an ascending traverse on greasy holds to finish over a small chockstone. (This pitch would be no trouble at all if the rocks were dry.)

A section of medium size boulders follows, leading in about 10 minutes to an enormous block almost filling the gorge, with a smaller boulder in front and difficult cracks to the left and right each with a small pool at the base. The best way to tackle this section is either by the groove against the left wall, or by means of a little chimney on the left between the large block and the subsidiary boulder in front. (If you try to get up on the right hand side of this boulder you are likely to run into trouble with a projecting chockstone at chest height.) If you choose the chimney then you have to go up an easy slab to the top of the big block from which there is a short easy descent on the other side.

An easier section of boulders and scree comes next, passing a side gully on the right, after which there is a varied stretch with 2 pitches easily climbed by sloping shelves on the left. The gorge then narrows again and is filled with a chaotic mass of huge blocks. On the right a red arrow indicates a fascinating through-route between a giant block and the right hand wall. After this only one more boulder gives a trifling difficulty before a path on the left hand side of the gorge avoids further problems and leads to the Entreforc.

Return, of course, the same way; slightly less strenuous going down!

Tunnel mouth - Narrows & 1st difficulty	35 mins.
Narrows - Top of difficult boulder	25 mins.
This boulder - side gully	15 mins.
Side gully - top difficult blocks	1hr.15mins.
Diff. blocks - Entreforc.	20mins.
Entreforc - Sa Calobra	c. 2hrs.40mins.

22. MASSANELLA

Massanella is the highest accessible peak in Mallorca since the Puig Mayor is prohibited. As such it is very popular and you can expect to meet other walkers especially on Sundays when Mallorquin walkers go out. The twin peaks at the top are visible from many places and make the mountain instantly recognisable. A freshwater spring not far below the summit, approached by stone steps leading down into a cave, is an attractive place especially on a hot day. The normal way is by a good path, but if there is snow on the ground it is not always easy to follow. The alternative route by the old pilgrim's way to the Coll des Prat

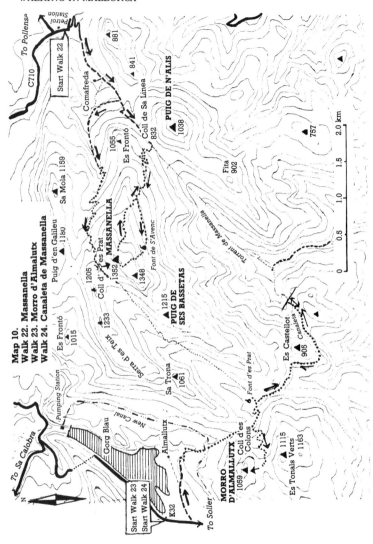

Map 10.
Walk 22. Massanella
Walk 23. Morro d'Almalutx
Walk 24. Canaleta de Massanella

involves a rock scramble and is only for those with suitable experience.

(a) **Normal way**

Starting point:　　　　Petrol station, Lluc.

Time:　　　　　　　5hr.

Distance:　　　　　　11km.

Height:　　　　　　　1352m.

Grade:　　　　　　　B+.

Map:　　　　　　　　Inca 1:50,000 or Selva 1:25,000.

There is a parking place by the petrol station on the C710 Lluc-Inca road between K14 and K15. Walk south from here towards Inca and go through the green gates on the right just across the bridge over the Torrent des Guix. Follow the unsurfaced track up to the *finca* Comafreda by taking the first turn right, or take a very steep short cut which begins on the right just as you go through the gate. After passing the farm, seen to the right, bear left at the side of a wall where a sign reads 'Puig de Massanella, Puig d'es Galileu, Puig d'en Ali'.

In about five minutes cross a stile over a wall, then bear right over a broken-down wall and follow the paint marks up through the woods until a wide track is met by a large boulder with a red paint mark. Follow this track to the Coll de sa Linea at 832m. and turn sharp right by the two indication stones. A good path leads up in zigzags through the trees and arrives at an engraved stone marking a bifurcation in the path. The left path is signposted 'Font y Puig' and the right one 'Puig y Font'. (A few metres below this there is a deep pit on the right of the path named the 'Avenc de Cami'.) Either route may be taken to the top by good well-marked paths, although the one to the right is slightly easier to follow. Going to the spring first is recommended as it makes a perfect place for a lunch stop. So take the left branch, at first through trees then on more open stony ground. In some places there are so many natural ledges that it is easy to mistake them for paths, so it is as well to watch out for paint marks and cairns. There is a large cairn marking the place where the path begins to rise up towards an isolated *alzine* or evergreen oak. Here marker stones have been cemented to the slabs to show the way. Above this a roughly horizontal section leads to the fountain, where water dripping down through the rocks collects in a series of stone troughs in the lower of two caves.

If you choose a weekday for this walk you may have this spot to yourself. On New Years Day 1985 we were kept company by a solitary alpine accentor very keen to accept offerings from our packed lunches. There was crisp snow on the ground and not much warmth in the sun, but it was a very quiet and pleasant place to be.

From the fountain the path continues horizontally for about 20m. before leading up a rocky staircase to the sloping shelf that lies below the summit. On this shelf another indication stone points the way to the top, near which is a very large snow-pit. On the summit there are the remains of an iron cross fixed to a rock-wall. To find the way down in mist or cloud, stand with your back to this and turn left! Normally it is possible to see the way down easy rocks until you can pick up the path on the sloping plain below. This path is easy to follow and leads to the bifurcation with a marker stone just above the Avenc de Cami, from where the route of ascent is followed back to the main road.

Lluc petrol station - Coll de sa Linia	1hr.
Coll de sa Linia - Sa Font de s'Avenc	1hr.
Sa Font - Massanella summit	45mins.
Massanella summit - Lluc petrol station	2hr.30mins.

(b) Ascent by the Coll des Prat

Starting point:	Lluc petrol station.
Time:	5hr.15min.
Distance:	12km.
Height:	1352m.
Grade:	A+.
Map:	Inca 1:50,000 or Selva 1:25,000.

Follow the normal way up for about 40 minutes until you meet the wide track by a large boulder with a red paint mark. Turn right here, passing a *sitja* on the left. Climb over a low wall at a barrier across the track and turn left to pass a spring. A good forest road leads up through the trees and where these thin out the old pilgrim's trail, still in good condition and easy to follow, leads right up to the top of the pass. There is a little confusion around some ruined buildings and snow-pits but it is easy enough to get to the pass, across which there is a wall. Turn left and go up by the wall and in to an obvious gully. Where this becomes steep traverse right until a way can be found up a steep but easy chimney, reaching the summit ridge about 20m. to the right of the top. Other ways up these rocks could easily be found: we observed a party of 6 descending slightly to the right (looking up) of our route.

Descent can be made either by the direct route described in 22(a) or by the Font de s'Avenc. The latter is recommended.

From the top follow the path slightly east of south to the lip of the sloping ledge down to the spring. The path from the Font de s'Avenc is well-marked, but there are places where it could be lost, so keep looking for cairns and red paint marks. If you go off the route you are likely to drop too low down and have to re-ascend steep ground at some point. This path leads to a junction with the other path that descends directly from the summit, at a marker stone just above the 'Avenc de Cami'. From here the path down to the Coll de sa Linia is unmistakable. At the col turn left and after about 15min. turn right at a boulder marked by a red paint dash. Now return by the route of ascent.

Petrol station, Lluc - Coll d'es Prat	2hr.15min.
Coll d'es Prat - Massanella	50min.
Massanella - Font de s'Avenc.	30min.
Font de s'Avenc - Coll de sa Linia	50min.
Coll de sa Linia - Lluc petrol station	50min.

23. MORRO D'ALMALLUTX

This is a short excursion in the Gorg Blau area, passing many interesting features and with excellent views of Massanella and the east side of the Puig Mayor. Although it is pathless at the top it is not difficult ground. The Morro d'Almallutx is one of a group of four peaks between the Massanella massif and the Sa Rateta-L'Ofre ridge. (See map 16.) The Tossals Vert (or Tonals Vert), 1115m, lies S.S.E. of the Morro d'Almallutx and could easily be climbed from the col between the two peaks.

Starting point:	K32, Pollensa - Soller road.
Time:	3hr.20min.
Distance:	8km.
Height:	1059m.
Grade:	B.
Map:	Soller 1:50,000 and Inca 1:50,000.

Park on the wide grass verge opposite K32 on the Pollensa-Soller road, just after passing the Gorg Blau reservoir. Walk up the road to the first gates on the left: this is the entrance to the *finca* Almallutx and there is a 'no entry' sign on the gate. The track leads down to the valley floor and makes a sharp bend to the right then goes through a gateway. Just beyond here a cairn on the right marks the beginning of a good path leading up through the woods, a little indistinct at first. This path passes several *sitjes* before leaving the woods for more open ground. This open ground is left almost opposite an old oven, which at first sight looks like a very large cairn, and the woods re-entered on the right. Soon the path crosses a modern aqueduct along which water is pumped from the Gorg Blau to the Cuber reservoir in a deep open channel. The path now goes through a narrow valley, rising slightly to the Coll d'es Coloms, which is reached shortly after passing through the second of two gateways. Where the path starts to level out, an enormous pointed rock can be glimpsed through the trees high up on the right. Keep the position of this in mind, in case you lose the path in the trees! This path begins about 20m. after the main path starts to descend, on the right hand side by a marker stone bearing the numbers 802,092. (The height of the Coll d'es Coloms is 822m.)

This path used to be a good one, but in 1985 the large numbers of fallen trees made it a bit difficult to follow. There are some cairns and some red paint marks, and the path soon passes an old lime kiln. About 20m. past a large boulder, the path crosses the valley to the left and eventually reaches the col between the Morro d'Almallutx and the the Tossals Vert. It passes quite close to the left hand side of the large pointed rock seen from below.

On the col there are the remains of an old *casa de sa neu* and a hut were the snow workers used to live while collecting the snow. From here turn right and go up easy rocks, almost bare of vegetation, to the top of the Morro d'Almallutx. Return is by the route of ascent.

K32 - Coll d'es Coloms	50min.
Coll d'es Coloms - Morro d'Almallutx	1hr.
Morro d'Almallutx - K32.	1hr.30min.

ARBUTUS UNEDO
(STRAWBERRY TREE)

Canaleta de Massanella (Walk 24)

24. CANALETA DE MASSANELLA

This old water-course provides a walk which is very spectacular and not at all strenuous, although it is somewhat exposed in places. The construction of this *canaleta* which takes water from the Font d'es Prat to Mancor del Valle was begun in 1748 and completed in two years. Before modernisation in 1983 when the water was piped, it used to flow in an open channel and must have been even more attractive than it is now. Access to the once freely-flowing water has thoughtfully been provided by taps at intervals along the pipeline, signposted *'Agua Potabile'*.

Starting point:	K32 on C710.
Time:	4hr.20min.
Distance:	12km.
Height:	822m. (Coll d'es Coloms) 839m.
Grade:	B.
Map:	Inca 1:50,000 or Selva 1:25,000 (N.B., starting point is on Soller 1:50,000).

Park on the grass opposite to K32 and follow the route up to the Coll d'es Coloms as in Walk 23. Follow the path down from the pass and after about ten minutes climb over a wooden stile. From here go straight on to reach the Font de Massanella (or Font d'es Prat) in a further five minutes. (Alternatively take the first narrow path on the left by a *sitja* to the old Es Prat farmhouse, from where there are good views, then bear right here to reach the spring.) The spring, situated in a pleasant open clearing, is covered over and gated. Cross the stream and follow down the left bank for about 300m to an open meadow where large clumps of a beautiful white flower, summer snowflake, grow in the pools of water fed by the stream. Here the *canaleta* begins, with the pipeline buried by earth and stones between the stone walls that used to bound the open channel. In about five minutes an arched aqueduct carries it across a ravine, then it continues along the side of the hill. Soon it goes round a corner by means of a tunnel, then drops down slightly to a wooded col at 708m., between Es Castellot and Mitjana. After this it falls more rapidly to the long valley which descends southwards from the col between Massanella and the Puig d'en Alis. Various paths will be seen on the left leading down into this valley, but the walk described here ends at a wall a little further on, after which the *canaleta* begins to plunge down more steeply. Return by the same route to the starting point.

Map 11. Walk 25. Sa Rateta and L'Ofre

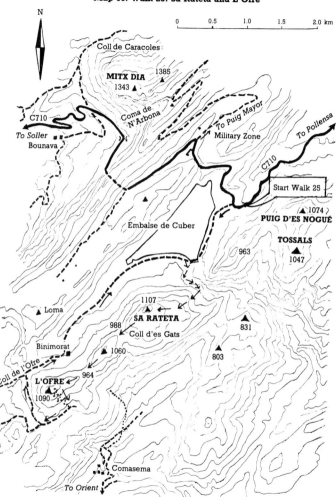

K32 - Coll d'es Coloms	50min.
Coll d'es Coloms - Font d'es Prat	15min.
Font d'es Prat - wall	1hr.10min.
Wall - Coll d'es Coloms	1hr.15min.
Coll d'es Coloms - K32.	50min.

25. SA RATETA AND L'OFRE

L'Ofre is most often climbed from Soller from where it is seen as a distinctive triangular peak. This walk approaches from the north-east, starting and finishing at the Embalse de Cuber *(Em-bal-say day Coo-bair)*, one of the main bird-watching sites where there is a chance of seeing ospreys fishing and many other birds. There is an enjoyable ridge walk from Sa Rateta to L'Ofre.

Starting point:	K34 on the C710 Pollensa-Soller road.
Time:	4hr.20min.
Distance:	8km.
Height:	1107m, 1060m, 1090m.
Grade:	B.
Map:	Soller 1:50,000.

Park at the entrance to the Cuber reservoir. There is an access gate for pedestrians at the side of the main locked gates; go through here and walk along the road to the dam. The next part of the route can be seen from the central turret at the right hand side of the dam. Looking south, a shallow rake will be observed above the midpoint between a water-pipe on the left and a stone wall on the right. This is most easily reached by turning left about 20m beyond the dam and following an indistinct path above, but fairly close to the stone wall. Follow this rake up towards the ridge, avoiding the main crags. After crossing a broken wall and fence, traces of an old path become more evident and lead into an easy gully which steepens a little towards the top. Go up this gully and at the top make for the ridge between two conspicuous trees, an evergreen oak and a pine. Just over the other side of the ridge is a hidden valley and natural ledges of rock and scree can be followed easily up to the head of this, to arrive at a plateau.

Swing round to the right and make for the top of Sa Rateta, where there is a summit book started by a group of Mallorquin walkers on 23rd December 1983. From here the ridge continues horizontally at first towards the south-west and then drops down quite steeply to the

Massanella from Rateta (Walk 25)

Coll d'es Gats (988m), with traces of a path. There is an unusual and conspicuous patch of short grass on this col. Going up the next ridge from here, the steep crag ahead is avoided by making for an obvious shelf on the left. Then easy rocks lead round behind the steep ground to rejoin the ridge. Continue over the unnamed top at 1060m to the 904m col before L'Ofre. (There is a way down into the Cuber valley from this col.) The L'Ofre ridge is gained by easy slabs to the left of the pylon, and a cairned path followed along to the top.

To descend, go back along the ridge for about 50m to a small shoulder and find the path down to the south, towards the Coll d'en Poma, marked by red paint marks at first. This path has many variations and is quite easy to lose, but it eventually arrives at flattish ground about 50m east of the wall which runs south from the foot of the rocks. The cart-track is reached in a couple of minutes from here. Turn right along this through a gap in the wall and follow it round to the west where it meets the track from the Cases de L'Ofre just before arriving at the Coll de L'Ofre where there is a large cairn. From here follow the track back through the valley to the road.

Cuber entrance - Sa Rateta	1hr.30min.
Sa Rateta - L'Ofre	1hr.15min.
L'Ofre - Col de L'Ofre	35min.
Coll de L'Ofre - Cuber entrance.	1hr.

ASPARAGUS ACUTITOLIUS

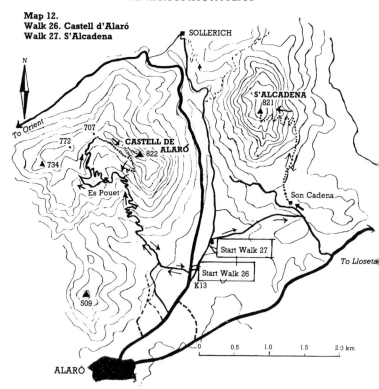

Map 12.
Walk 26. Castell d'Alaró
Walk 27. S'Alcadena

26. CASTELL D'ALARÒ, OR GARITA

Garita, or the Puig d'Alarò, is one of the two 'sugar loaf' mountains seen on the west of the Inca-Palma road. (The other is Alcadena, Walk no.27). The Castell d'Alarò formerly covered almost all the top of the mountain and the approaches to it are well-defended by steep cliffs. This is a pleasant easy walk up an unsurfaced road to a high col at 707m from where a good path leads along the base of the cliffs and then up steps and ramps to the gated entrance of the castle.

Starting point:	K13 on the Alarò-Orient road.
Time:	3.5hr.
Distance:	8.9km.
Height:	822m.
Grade:	C.
Map:	Alarò 1:25,000, or Soller 1:50,000.

A car may be left on a wide grassy verge quite near the K13 stone where the walk begins. Turn left a few metres further on towards Orient at a track signposted 'Castillo. Es Pouet'. (Alternatively you can drive up this track for c.0.5km and park on waste ground on the left, just before the gateway where the road becomes an unsurfaced track.) Here it should be pointed out that this track is used by cars up to the Restaurant Es Pouet and right on up to the col and this is a popular outing for local people especially at weekends: better to do this walk midweek.

There are three short-cuts which avoid the road and make use of an old mule-track, winding up through terraces of olive trees. All are marked with red painted arrows and are easy to follow, the first one starting by some big boulders at the second gateway. After the Restaurant Es Pouet the main track keeps to the left, but you can find various alternatives on the right. At the col there is a picnic place under the trees, from where the path to the castle goes up by a wall, waymarked by a yellow painted arrow. It is a well-built path with steps and the protection of a fence in places. In 10-15 minutes it joins another path at a signpost which directs you left to the 'Castillo'. (The path to the right leads back to Alarò and is the route of descent.) From here it is another 5 mins to the Castle which is entered by a gatehouse with a metal gate. There are extensive views from the ruins, over the plains to the bay of Palma and north and west over the Orient valley to the Sierra de Tramuntana. From the castle it is 10 minutes to the top of Garita where there is a small bar-restaurant in the style of an alpine hut, where coffee, wine and food may be ordered at very reasonable prices.

The return is by the same way back to the castle and down to the path junction already mentioned. The Alaró path joins the route of ascent at a point by-passed by a short-cut on the way up.

K13. - Summit	2hr.
Summit - K13.	1.5hr.

27. S'ALCADENA

The massif of S'Alcadena is on the east of the Alaró-Orient road, opposite the Castell d'Alaró (Walk 26). It is a striking mountain from all directions, being defended on all sides by vertical cliffs. This walk utilises the one line of weakness on the east side. The approach is by a private road through the grounds of the *finca* Son Cadena where you are very likely to meet the owner working in his fields. A few minutes conversation is customary and he will probably enquire where you are going and be helpful in pointing out the way. Some rudimentary knowledge of the language is a help, as he speaks no English.

Starting point:	K13, Alaró-Orient road (PM 210).
Time:	4hr.10min.
Distance:	8km.
Height:	817m.
Grade:	B+.
Map:	Soller 1:50,000 & Inca 1:50,000 or Alaró 1:25,000 + Inca 1:25,000.

A car may be left on the grass verge fairly near the K13 stone on the Alaró-Orient road where the walk begins. Walk towards Orient and fork right at a bend in the road. Take the second turn right down a narrow lane with a stone barn on the corner and then cross the Solleric stream by a ford. (No water, normally.) The gates of the *finca* Son Cadena are soon reached and the track followed up to the farm buildings. At the house turn right through a gate, then left round the back of the house. Here turn right up a well-laid cobbled track which leads through olive terraces to the east side of the mountain and eventually through a gate. Go through the gate, turn left and then almost immediately right. This path continues to contour along the east side of the mountain through cultivated terraces and then into a wood of evergreen oaks and pines. After going through another gateway with a boulder at the right hand side the path begins to rise

Castell d'Alaró (Walk 26)

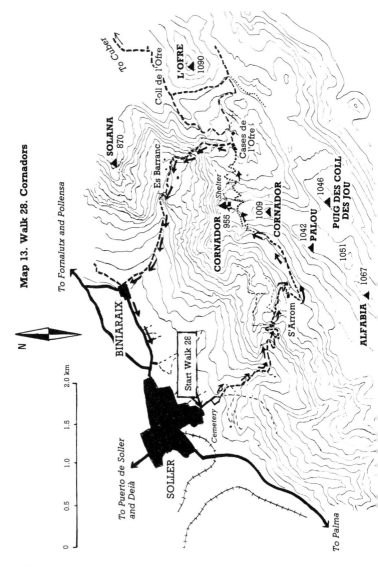

Map 13. Walk 28. Cornadors

more steeply and there are some cairns. Soon a very old gate between high stone gateposts topped with wooden beams is reached; this is the only access to the normal way up the mountain.

The route now goes up a wide gully by a well-constructed path. At one point this has collapsed, but this presents no real difficulty. After emerging on a shoulder the path ascends gradually to the south to arrive at a *sitja*. From here there is no path and it is quite rough going up fairly steep tree-covered ground to the top, which lies roughly in line with the gully up which the path came. Other *sitjes* and traces of paths will be found but none of the latter are much use in getting to the top. It is essential to return by the same route.

K13 - Son Cadena	40min.
Son Cadena - *sitja*	1hr.10min.
Sitja - summit	40min.
Summit - Son Cadena	1hr.
Son Cadena - K13	40min.

28. CORNADORS

This popular walk from Soller is both easy and spectacular. Almost entirely on cart tracks and good well-made paths, there are no real difficulties, but it does involve an ascent of about 900m. The descent is by part of the old pilgrims' route from Soller to Lluc, still known locally as the 'Pilgrim steps'. All the way down the *barranc* to Biniaraix it is a beautifully constructed path with laid stones and steps. The views are good all the way and the outlook from the Mirador de l'Ofre near the top of Cornadors is particularly impressive.

Starting point:	Soller railway station.
Time:	5hr.30min.
Distance:	16km.
Height:	955m.
Grade:	C+.
Map:	Soller 1:25,000 or Soller 1:50,000.

From the station, facing downhill towards the church, turn first right along a narrow street in front of the Hotel Guia. Take the first turn right again, second left, then first right again. Keep along this road (the Calle de Pablo Noguera) until the cemetery is passed on the right. Just past the cemetery take a left fork, then in two minutes a right fork which crosses the stream by a bridge. In a further two minutes the route turns sharp left at a fork with the minor track going off to the

right. After this it is a question of keeping to the main track, marked here and there by small red paint marks. The track is a well-maintained one and leads up through old olive terraces and then into a forest of evergreen oaks where old *sitjes* and lime-ovens will be noticed.

After about 1hr.30min. go through a gate to meet another track at a T-junction and turn right. There is a blue painted sign here pointing back to Soller, useful if you are doing this walk in reverse. After five minutes or so go through a metal gate and take a right fork. The high farmhouse S'Arrom is now in sight on a plateau and the track swings left, then zigzags up an attractive narrow gully to reach it. On the way up here watch out for some steps on the left leading to an access gate, as the double gates on the track are usually locked. When S'Arrom is reached, follow the track round to the left, then right again past the house to the south. Here there is an engraved stone sign with the word 'MIRADOR' and an arrow pointing to some stone steps. These steps and the path ahead lead to an old well in a tunnel, the 'Font de ses Piquetes', the water in which looks very uninviting. After reaching the well, scramble up the hillside above it to regain the cart track. If you are descending this way, there is another engraved stone on the track at this point. In about another 10 minutes, the track does a sharp bend to the right, where there is yet another stone. After this it becomes a narrow path which soon climbs in zigzags up a sloping shelf to a col, where a high fence is crossed by a stile. The *rifugio* is in sight here and is reached in a further 15 minutes, after turning left at the col between the two tops of Cornadors.

The stone shelter has a sound roof and stone benches. It is maintained, as is the Mirador, by the *Fomento del Turismo*. From the shelter it is only a few minutes to the 955m top of Es Cornadors and then down to the Mirador overlooking the *barranc*. The other top of Cornadors can easily be reached from the col between the two tops, allowing an extra 20 minutes for this. To continue this walk, go back from the *rifugio* to the col between the tops and turn left down to the houses on the tiny green plateau of L'Ofre. Go through the field gate and follow the path to a large barn with painted signs on the walls. These point right to 'L'Ofre Mirador, Soller 8km' and left '27km Lluc, Por favor, No acampar, TOROS*. Just past the barn, turn left off the main track to Lluc, where there is a sign to Soller. This path is the old pilgrims' way and is the only way down the *barranc* or gorge. About 50 minutes after leaving the plateau the path arrives at the corner of a wall, where a painted arrow points out the way up. If doing this walk in reverse, take care to find this as the steps and path to the

L'Ofre from Cornador (Walk 28)   109

Cornadors from el barranc (Walk 28)

left lead eventually into a steep and rather loose gully.

Continue down the main track which goes through a narrow shaded cleft and crosses the stream several times, with both bridges and stepping stones provided. Near Biniaraix the path joins another track at a gate with a 'No entry' sign and another sign which reads 'L'Ofre, Lluc a peu'**. Once in the village, follow the road back to Soller. To return to the station, go up the hill to the right of the church from the main square, the Plaza de la Constitucion. (In Biniaraix there is a bar on the left of the main street where the most delicious fresh orange juice is squeezed out from an endless supply of the local fruit.)

Soller station - S'Arrom	2hr.
S'Arrom - Cornadors	1hr.
Cornadors - Cases de L'Ofre	35min.
Cases de L'Ofre - Biniaraix	1hr.35min.
Biniaraix - Soller station	30min.

* Toros = Bulls.   ** Lluc a peu = Lluc on foot.

QUERCUS ILEX (HOLM OAK)

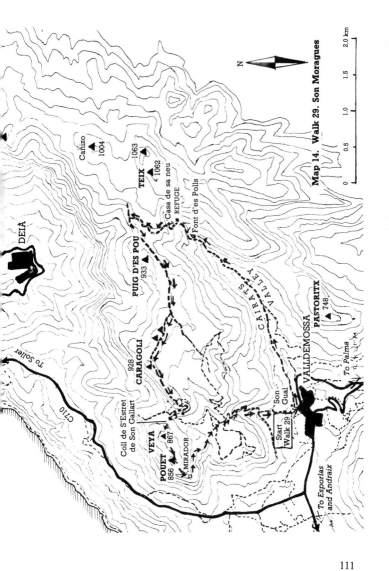

Map 14. Walk 29. Son Moragues

Pilgrim Steps, near Bianaritx (Walk 28)

29. SON MORAGUES, THE CAMINO DEL ARCHIDUQUE AND TEIX

This walk from Valldemossa is quite long and strenuous but so full of interest it can claim to be one of the best on the island. Son Moragues is a *finca* of Valldemossa bought by ICONA in 1979 and turned over to public use. It is a centre of nature conservation and there are strict rules such as no dogs, no rubbish, and no fires from 1st June until 30th October. One of the main attractions is the wonderful path which the Archduke Luis Salvador had constructed along the edge of a high plateau overlooking the sea. Another is the wooded Cairats valley where ICONA have provided what amounts to an open-air museum, with restorations of lime-kilns, a snow-house and a *sitja* with logs piled up ready for charcoaling. The little booklet published by ICONA has illustrations of these and of the flora and fauna and is well worth obtaining if you come across any on sale. (See bibliography, p.141)

Starting point:	Son Gual, Valldemosssa.
Time:	6hr.15min.
Distance:	16km.
Height:	1,062m.
Grade:	B+.
Map:	Soller 1:50,000 or Esporlas 1:25,000 & Alaró 1:25,000.

It is easy to shorten this walk, either by missing out Teix or by taking one of the short cuts back to Es Pouet, of which the first is the easiest to follow.

Park in the main car park on the outskirts of Valldemossa, or in the new estate to the N.E. of the town behind the large towered house Son Gual.

Walk along the road past Son Gual (at first parallel to the main road), which soon leads north-east into the Cairats valley. The former forest road used by the charcoal burners is now unfortunately rather a wide and stony track, easy to follow but not too pleasant to walk on, the price paid for the otherwise excellent job done by the Conservationists in restoring the various buildings and sites in this area.

The Font d'es Poll or Poplars' Well is an attractive place for a short rest in hot weather, but 10 minutes further on is the excellent stone shelter provided for walkers by ICONA. This is equipped with tables and benches and has an enormous fireplace across one corner: the walls are decorated with coloured posters showing the plants and animals etc. The hut was originally the living quarters of the *nevaters* or snow workers, and the *casa de sa neu* or snow-house itself is a few minutes further on: an enormous pit 24m x 8m. It is at a height just below 800m.

The road ends here and the walk continues along the footpath constructed by the archduke and recently restored by ICONA. A signpost soon points the way to the summit of Teix on the right. (About 2km there and back and about 220m of ascent - allow c.1¼-1½ hours extra.)

The archduke's path continues onwards and soon passes a mirador overlooking Deiá and the coast, then crosses a flat area, the 'Pla dets Aritges', where it becomes a little indistinct. The direction here is almost due west. After about 40 minutes past the Teix summit path a cairn marks the branch path to the left which can be followed down to Es Pouet if you wish to shorten the walk. Once past here the path becomes built up again and is very easy to follow. It swings towards the Puig Caragoli and then left along the very edge of the cliffs. The path was built so that the duke could walk along this potentially dangerous place while still enjoying the view and it is possible to do just this for hundreds of metres. There is no fence or other protection against the drop but the path is a wide one and there is no danger. Soon the path descends towards a wooded pass, the Coll de S'Estret de Son Gallart. By some stone seats another path on the left leads down to

Es Pouet, and in a further few minutes there is a cross path with that on the left again going to Es Pouet and that on the right to Deiá. After 10 minutes from the cross path bear left, the path on the right dropping down to Deiá. Follow the cairns and paint marks upwards to reach an old stone shelter near the top of Veyá at 876m. From the shelter continue along the wooded ridge, passing a trig point and keeping to the path, which is again built up here and easy to find in spite of being a little overgrown with trees. The path leads to the Mirador de Ses Puntes, where there is yet another impressive view.

From the Mirador, turn left along the path leading to Es Pouet passing a number of *sitjes* by one of which is an old oven. At Es Pouet, go straight on past the well (which unfortunately is polluted) and in 5 minutes come to a clearing on some level ground. Go straight on again and climb a gate in a stone wall, then in another 10 minutes go straight on at a cross path. The whole area is riddled with paths, but now you are on an obvious charcoal-burners route and it goes down through the forest where you will see many *sitjes*. Look out for the red paint signs and continue down hill to reach a broken gate. Climb this and keep going until you meet a wider track. Turn right here and follow this track back to Son Gual.

Son Gual - ICONA shelter	1hr.
ICONA shelter - Estret de Son Gallart	1hr.50min.
Estret - Veyá shelter	20min.
Veyá shelter - Mirador de ses Puntes	30min.
Mirador - Es Pouet	20min.
Es Pouet - Son Gual	1hr.

30. GALATZÓ

Galatzó is the highest peak in the south-western mountains and the only one over 1,000m in this area. It is seen as a prominent pyramid from many parts of the island. The most usual way up is from Son Fortuny near Estellencs by a very good path and it can also be climbed from Puigpunent or Galilea. The way up described here is not so well known but is an interesting route when combined with a descent by the Son Fortuny path. The only disadvantage is having to walk about 4km along the road at the end of the day. If you are with friends and have two cars it is worth leaving one in Estellencs.

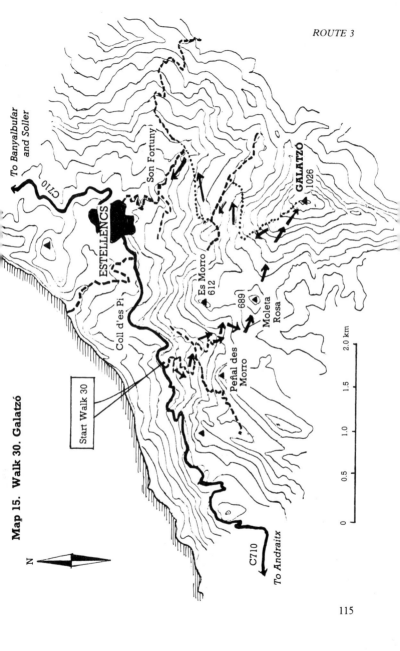

Map 15. Walk 30. Galatzó

N

Start Walk 30

To Banyalbufar and Soller

C710

ESTELLENCS

Son Fortuny

GALATZÓ
1026

Coll d'es Pi

Es Morro
612

689

Moleta
Rosa

Peñal des
Morro

C710

To Andraitx

0   0.5   1.0   1.5   2.0 km

Starting point:	K97, Estellencs-Andraitx road.
Time:	5hr.40min.
Distance:	11km.
Height:	1,026m.
Grade:	B+.
Map:	Dragonera 1:25,000 and Esporles 1:25,000. (Both very inaccurate.)

A track leaves the Estellencs-Andraitx road on the left just by K97 and it is possible to leave a small car a few metres up here. After about 15 minutes walk another track is met at a T-junction. Turn left (east) here until a little path is seen on the right (south-east) leading into a narrow valley. At this point two streams meet. The path leads at first up the right hand stream bed. Very soon look for a way on the left which leads across a scree slope into the other valley. There is another path here which can be followed up towards the head of the valley. When this steepens, go up obliquely to the right and a short easy scramble leads up onto a small plateau between the Peñal des Morro and the Moleta Rasa. The traces of path now become confused with animal tracks but it is not difficult to pick a way up the gently rising ridge to the top of the Moleta Rasa (689m).

From this top, go down the little escarpment by an easy rock groove and on down to the Coll de Sa Moleta Rasa, where a few pine trees provide welcome shade on hot days. From the col there is a cairned way up some bare rock ribs sloping up first to the left and then back right to reach the ridge again by some pines. After this the way goes up a wide valley on the left of the ridge, making for a broad gully on the left of an obvious steep crag. Once in the gully the path becomes better and continues up to the top. About 5-10 minutes before the top, a summit book is hidden under a large painted boulder. Paint signs show the way from here up the steepish rocks to the summit of Galatzó.

The way down to Son Fortuny is easy to find, being a good path well supplied with cairns and red paint signs. It diverges from the ascent route at the bottom of the broad gully and after 10 minutes reaches a large white rock where red paint arrows point to the way up. The path turns sharp right here and continues horizontally before descending to a small hut. There are two paths here. Take the left one and after about 3 minutes turn right at a cairn. A series of zigzags leads down into a gully and part way down a paint mark indicates another right turn at a T-junction. The path then goes through a rock cutting to enter a wide wooded valley, where it makes a gradual descent to a large *sitja*. Here the path turns sharp left and goes down through the forest with cairns or paint marks showing the route. At one point, well down the valley, a new track crosses the path at an open clearing and the way down is not too clear at first. Turn right at a large cairn, then left at a red paint sign where the old path can be picked up again. This old path is laid with cobbles here and leads down to the large *finca* of Son Fortuny, from where the farm track is followed down to the road. Alternatively a short cut can be taken from about half way down, where a field path leads down the side of a stream and then crosses it to reach the old houses of Estellencs.

K97 - Moleta Rasa top	1hr.20min.
Moleta Rasa - Galatzó	1hr.40min.
Galatzó - Son Fortuny	1hr.40min.
Son Fortuny - Estellencs	20min.
Estellencs-K97	40min.

ASHPODELUS ALBUS

APPENDIX 1. ALPHABETICAL REFERENCE SECTION

Banks There are several banks in most of the main resorts, but only one in Cala San Vicente. Opening hours are 09.00 to 14.00 but they may also close for lunch from 11.30 to 12.30. There are fairly frequent holidays when the banks close all day and most hotel notice boards will give this information. In 1985 the banks accepted English cheques backed by a cheque card. One advantage of this system is that it seems to take several weeks before the money is deducted from your account. In 1986 a new system was in operation and it is recommended that Eurocheques and a Eurocheque card are obtained before setting out, although it is possible that your normal cheques may still be acceptable. Travellers' cheques can be exchanged at most hotels and travel agencies displaying a *cambio* sign, but the exchange rate is usually less favourable than that in the banks. Passports must be shown when exchanging money or cheques.

Bus travel Although the walker is strongly advised to hire a car for getting to the starting point of the walks, there may be occasions when it is desirable to use public transport and a knowledge of the services available would not come amiss. If you are intending to use these services at all then it is advisable to obtain up-to-date timetables when you arrive on the island. The best place to ask for one is at a bus station, rather than a tourist office. Many of the services are locally organised though, and you cannot for example obtain a timetable for the Puerto Pollensa-Ca'n Picafort route from the Pollensa bus station because it is operated by a different company. Timetables are usually posted up by the bus stops, and couriers in the hotels have the details in their information books or on their notice boards.

The following timetables were operating in winter 1984-85 and will give an indication of the frequency and times, but of course these may be changed at any time. More buses run in the summer, which is roughly the beginning of May to the end of September, but vary according to the bus company, the weather, and the demand. At present walkers are badly served by the buses, but perhaps if more walkers create a demand something will be done about it. What is particularly needed is a morning bus from Pollensa to Lluc or even better to Soller, and an evening bus in the reverse direction. At present (1985) there is a morning bus from Soller along the C710 with a return in the evening, which is alright if you are based in Soller, but even this is only run at weekends in the winter. (See P.124)

There are many buses from Palma radiating in all directions for which details can easily be obtained if you are staying in Palma. Most walkers will be based in the north of the island so only timetables relevant to this area are included here.

Timetables (N.B. These are 1985 timetables. Readers are reminded they may be changed at any time.)

Airport - Palma For those who book flight only it is useful to know that an airport bus runs into the Plaza España in Palma, right to the bus station where buses leave for the north and near the railway station. The buses leave on the hour every hour.

Palma - Pollensa - Puerto Pollensa The bus stop in Palma is in the bus station next to the Inca railway station in the Plaza España.

	Monday - Saturday				Sundays/Holidays		
Palma	10.00	13.30	17.30	19.15	10.00	16.30	20.30
Pollensa	11.00	14.30	18.30	20.15	11.00	17.30	21.30
Puerto Pol.	11.15	14.45	18.45	20.30	11.15	17.45	21.45
Puerto Pol.	07.15	09.00	14.00	17.30	08.00	14.45	18.45
Pollensa	07.30	09.15	14.15	17.45	08.15	15.00	19.00
Palma	08.30	10.15	15.15	18.45	09.15	16.00	20.00

Pollensa - Puerto Pollensa There is a bus station in Pollensa. The bus stop in Puerto Pollensa is on the sea-front opposite the bar YUM-YUM. It is a fairly frequent service and the journey takes 15 minutes. Only the starting times are given.

Pollensa - Puerto Weekdays								
6.45	07.30	08.15	09.30	10.15	11.10	12.00	13.00	13.30
14.30	15.45	16.15	17.00	17.45	18.30	19.15	20.15	
Sundays/Holidays								
07.30	08.30	09.30	10.15	11.10	12.00	13.00	14.15	16.00
16.30	17.00	17.30	18.15	19.15	20.15	21.30		

Map 17.
PALMA City Centre

0   100   200   300   400   500   600m

Puerto - Pollensa Weekdays
07.15 08.30 09.00 10.00 11.00 11.45 12.45 13.15 14.00 15.00 16.00 16.45 17.30 18.00 19.00 19.30 20.45
Sundays/Holidays
08.00 08.45 10.00 11.00 11.45 12.45 13.15 14.45 16.15 16.45 17.45 18.45 19.45 20.45 21.45

Pollensa - Cala San Vicente In Cala San Vicente the bus stop is outside the Bar Miguel in the Calle Temporal, not far from the bank. The bus also picks up at the Don Pedro, but at busy times it is best to walk up to the bus stop.

Pollensa - Cala San Vicente
Weekdays: 8.15 11.15 14.50 18.30 Holidays: 09.30 12.15 16.30
Cala San Vicente - Pollensa
Weekdays: 08.45 12.30 14.45 18.45 Holidays: 10.00 12.30 17.30

ARISARUM VULGARE

Puerto Pollensa - Alcudia - Ca'n Picafort This service is especially useful to bird watchers as it passes three major habitats: Albufereta, the Tucan Pool and the Albufera. This is a winter timetable, from 1 November to 31 March.

Pto.Poll.		10.30	12.45	15.30	17.30
Alcudia	09.25	10.45	13.00	15.45	17.45
Pto.Alcudia	09.30	10.50	13.05	15.50	17.50
Tucan	09.35	10.55	13.10	15.55	17.55
Ciudad Lagos	09.40	11.00	13.15	16.00	18.00
Ca'n Picafort	09.55	11.15	13.30	16.15	18.15
* *
Ca'n Picafort	09.45	12.00	14.45	16.45	18.15
Ciudad Lagos	10.00	12.15	13.00	17.00	18.30
Tucan	10.05	12.20	15.05	17.05	18.35
Pto.Alcudia	10.10	12.25	15.10	17.10	18.40
Alcudia	10.15	12.30	15.15	17.15	**18.45**
Pto.Poll.	10.30	12.45	15.30	17.30	

CERATONIA SILIQUA (HOCUST BEAN TREE)

Palma - Valldemossa - Deià - Puerto Soller This service could be very useful to walkers based in Soller but unfortunately the most important bus only runs in summer, in this case from 1 April to 30 September. This is the 09.30 from Puerto Soller, reaching Deià at 10.00 and Valldemossa at 10.30. However, walkers based in or near Palma can use it to get to Valldemossa or Soller. In Palma tickets can be obtained from the Bar Ca'n Meca in the Calle Archiduque Luis Salvador and the bus leaves from the other side of the block in the Calle 31 de Diciembre. (See plan, Map 17.) The bus stop at Puerto Soller is on the quay, but if you are getting on it at Soller it is important to know that the stop is in the Plaza America and not near the railway station.

Winter service 1 October - 30 March				
Palma	10.00	12.00*	15.00	19.00
Valldemossa	10.30	12.30*	15.30	19.30
Deià	10.45	12.45*	15.45	19.45
Puerto Soller	11.15	13.15*	16.15	20.15
* *				
Puerto Soller	07.30	14.30	16.00*	17.30
Deià	08.00	15.00	16.30*	18.00
Valldemossa	08.20	15.30	17.00*	18.30
Palma	08.50	16.00	17.30	19.00

* Not on Sundays and holidays.

Summer service from 1 April to 30 September					
Palma	07.45	10.00	12.00	16.15	19.30
Valldemossa	08.15	10.30	12.30	16.45	20.00
Deià	08.30	10.45	12.45	17.00	20.15
Puerto Soller	09.00	11.15	13.15	17.30	20.45
* *					
Puerto Soller	07.30	09.30	14.30	16.00	18.00
Deiá	08.00	10.00	15.00	16.30	18.30
Valldemossa	08.20	10.30	15.30	17.00	19.00
Palma	08.50?	11.00	16.00	17.30	19.30

Soller - Puerto Pollensa As mentioned earlier, this is an important bus for walkers staying in Soller. In summer it is a daily service but only runs at weekends in winter, approximately from 1 October to about Easter. This bus stop is outside the railway station in Soller.

Soller	09.00	19.25
Puerto Soller	09.30	19.10
Ses Barques	09.45	18.50
Army Base	10.05	18.35
Escorca	10.20	18.20
Lluc	10.35	18.00
Pollensa	11.20	17.20
Cala San Vicente	11.30	17.10
Puerto Pollensa	11.45	17.00

Car Hire Some package holidays offer free or reduced car hire as part of the deal, especially during the winter months. If this does not apply, then it is cheaper to hire locally than to book a car in advance with one of the international companies. The smallest and cheapest cars are the Seat Pandas, which are good for driving along the narrow mountain roads, but sometimes have starting problems. Note that the spare wheel, jack and wheel brace are under the front bonnet. A full current driving licence, international driving permit and passport are normally asked for when hiring a car.

Chemists The sign for a chemists shop is a green cross. Many medicines for which a prescription would be required in Great Britain can be bought over the counter. Staff are usually very helpful. There is a chemist in Puerto Pollensa near the junction of the Pollensa road with the coast road, and three in Pollensa, one being near the bus station.

Complaints All hotels, shops, bars and garages are compelled by law to have a supply of a complaints form *hoja de reclamaciones* (pronounced 'O-ha day-rek-lam-ath-i-o-nes'). These are for very serious complaints and should only be resorted to after every attempt has been made to get things put right in a friendly way. If a polite approach to manager or owner has not worked, then simply asking for the form may bring about a dramatic change of attitude as it is a very serious matter to have a complaint registered. The forms are in triplicate: one copy for the offending concern, one to be sent to the Oficina de Turismo, Avenida Jaime III, Palma, and one copy to be kept.

Currency The monetary unit is the *peseta (pta)*. There are coins of 1, 5, 25, 50 and 100 pesetas and banknotes of 100, 200, 500, 1,000 and 5,000 pesetas. A 5-peseta coin is called a *duro*. *During 1984-1985, the rate of exchange has varied between 190 and 210 pesetas to one pound sterling, so that an easy rule of thumb is 200 pesetas = £1.00. (20 pta = 10p, 50 pta = 25p, 1000 pta = £5.00 etc.).*

Drinks There are no 'licensing laws' as in Britain and there are very many bars where drinks are served all day. All supermarkets and nearly all village shops sell alcoholic drinks which are very good value at about 60 pta to some very expensive vintage wines at all prices. Wines in hotels and restaurants average 400 pta or about £2.00 per bottle. Some good Mallorquin wines are Felanitx Tinto and Franje Roja. Beer, *cerveza* (pronounced 'thair-bay-tha') is generally good. Draught is *de barril* or *a presion.* It may be more expensive than the wine. The Spanish coñac is good and not expensive at about 380 pta per bottle. Fundador and Carlos IV can be recommended.

Driving Getting to the start of the walks often means driving along narrow winding roads. The roads themselves are mainly good, but there can be problems when coaches going in the opposite direction are met with. The drivers are always very good and expert at edging past with only an inch or two to spare, but if this sort of thing worries you then avoid places like the Corniche road on the west coast and the Formentor peninsular on the days coaches go there. (Study the notice board in your hotel or ask a courier.)

Driving offences The traffic police are very strict and on-the-spot fines of the order of 1600-2400 pta are quite common. It is as well to be aware of the following Spanish laws:

1. Always use the seat belts.
2. Always indicate you are pulling out when overtaking anything, even parked cars, and allow 1m clearance.
3. Always dip headlights when coming up behind another vehicle as well as when approaching.
4. Pay particular attention to all *ceda el paso* (give way) signs and to Stop signs. Some road junctions can be confusing, but 'Stop means Stop' as a traffic policeman said to me when charging an

on-the-spot fine at the Tucan crossroads near Alcudia. (There is a STOP sign at a minor road, then a *ceda el paso* sign at a major road.)

5. Give way to all vehicles coming from the right.
6. Keep to the speed limit of 110km on C roads and 90km per hour on other roads, or other speed as shown locally.
7. Never cross unbroken white lines in the centre of the road. 'No overtaking' signs back up these white lines.
8. Do not park facing oncoming traffic or within 3m. of a corner.
9. Obey the priority signs on narrow roads and bridges. You have priority at a square sign with a white arrow pointing up, but must give way at a round sign with a red arrow pointing up.
10. Each car in Spain should carry a set of spare bulbs, but hire car companies do not provide these. If you are stopped at night with one of your lights out an instant fine will be applied but will be refunded or paid for by the company.

If you are stopped by the police for any offence whatsoever it is no use pleading ignorance of the law and highly inadvisable to argue. The best course of action is to apologise; *lo siento* or *lo mucho siento*. If it is not a very serious offence then you may be let off with a warning, but it is far more likely that you will be charged and required to pay a fine *(una multa)*. If this is the case you will be given a slip of paper explaining in English (or other non-Spanish language) what is to happen. The policeman booking you will then fill in a form describing the offence and ask you to sign it. He will sign it too and give you a copy to keep.

Food   See also markets and restaurants.

Mallorquin cuisine is similar to that of Catalonia on the mainland. Fish dishes are a speciality and so are *tapas* or wonderful titbits served with drinks in many bars. You may find the food in your hotel is rather too bland, as they are catering for all tastes, but you may be interested to sample some of the following dishes, both local and Spanish, when you have the opportunity:

Angulas: small eels fried whole in batter.

Arroz brut: rice soup with meat.

Bacalao: dried codfish cooked with tomatoes in a casserole.

Butifarra: Catalan spiced sausage, usually served with mushrooms.

Calamares: squid. Usually served *a la romana* or deep fried, in rings.

Caldera de peix: fish soup with rice and slices of bread.

Capo a lo Rei en Jaume: capon, cock or turkey stuffed with marzipan and sweet potatoes and slightly fried.

Caracoles: snails cooked in a garlic mayonnaise sauce.

Chorizo: a strong spicy sausage.

Coca mallorquin: a kind of pizza, often with fish.

Empanada: meat and vegetable pie.

Ensaimada: a very light flaky bun sprinkled with icing sugar, often eaten for breakfast or taken out as picnic food.

Escaldums: A casserole dish based on chicken pieces and potatoes in an almond sauce.

Espinagada: A savoury pie of eels and highly seasoned vegetables.

Frito Mallorquin: A fry-up of liver, kidneys, green peppers etc.

Gambas: prawns.

Gazpacho: a cold soup made from tomatoes, onions, peppers, cucumbers, garlic, oil and vinegar.

Graixonere: fish with vegetables and eggs.

Greixera: eggs and meat with artichokes, peas, beans, and herbs.

Guisantes a la catalana: peas fried with ham and onions.

Langosta a la Catalana: lobster sautéed in wine and rum with herbs and spices.

Lechona asada: roast sucking-pig.

Lenguado: sole, usually grilled with fresh herbs.

Mejillones a la marinera: mussels cooked in a very tasty sauce.

Pa amb oli: bread spread with oil and topped with ham and tomatoes.

Paella: one of the most famous Spanish dishes, popular at lunchtime. The best are cooked to order and take at least half an hour. It is a combination of rice with peas, onions, tomatoes, peppers and garlic and various seafoods, poultry and pork. Normally served in an iron dish straight from the oven.

Paella catalana: spicy sausages, pork, squid, tomato, chilli pepper and   peas.

Paella marinera: fish and seafood only.

Paella valenciana: the traditional dish with chicken, mussels, shrimp, prawns, peas, tomatoes and garlic.

Salmonetes: red mullet.

Sobrasada: pork-liver sausage, bright red with pimento.

Sopa mallorquina: a very filling soup, almost a stew, made from garlic, onions, vegetables in season and bread.

Tortilla españolo: omelette with potatoes.

Trempo: a summer salad with mixed vegetables.

Trucha a la navarra: trout filled with smoked ham or bacon.

Tumbet: A type of *ratatouille* with aubergines, peppers, potatoes and tomatoes cooked in olive oil.

Zarzuela: A mixture of various fish in a hot spicy sauce.

Markets   If you are self-catering you will enjoy buying fresh fruit and vegetables at the street markets. Even if you are staying at a hotel with full board you may like to supplement your packed lunches with some extra fruit and in any case it is a colourful and entertaining event. Most of the traders are strictly honest and prices are displayed everywhere, but it helps to learn enough numbers to do some simple arithmetic. Mistakes can be made and if you can point out you have been charged for a kilo of something instead of a media kilo, for example, then this can be rectified. Markets are also a good place to buy other goods, such as leather ware, carved wooden bowls, hand-painted fans, pottery or embroidered linen.

The main markets are as follows:

Alcudia:	Tuesday and Sunday
Inca:	Thursday
Palma:	Saturday
Pollensa:	Sunday
Puerto Pollensa:	Wednesday

Hotels often organise trips to the markets at Inca and Palma. Alcudia and Pollensa are easily reached by car or by public transport. The fruit and vegetable market in Pollensa is in the main square and the other market is in a big square a few minutes walk away. You must go in the morning as they all pack up about lunchtime.

Medical matters   Before setting out, or rather when booking your holiday, make sure that you have adequate insurance cover just to be on the safe side. If you are intending to go rock-climbing rather than walking, then read the small print in any insurance document to make sure that 'mountaineering' is not excluded, or take out a British Mountaineering Council Insurance policy or a policy with one of the other specialist Insurers.

There are doctors in all towns and a hospital in Palma, which can be reached in under two hours from the most distant parts of the island. It is not necessary to take an enormous supply of contingency medicines with you as anything you may require can easily be obtained. (See Chemists.) Personally I think it is worth taking a few simple items like anadins, throat tablets, indigestion tablets as well as elastoplast and something to relieve insect bites. Sun-protection cream, is on sale at nearly every shop. If you do have any medical emergency, then ask a courier, hotel staff, police or a tourist office where to go for help or to get a doctor.

Photography Bring all the film that you are likely to need with you as it is a lot more expensive to buy in Mallorca. Processing is also more expensive, but it may be worth having one film developed so that you have a chance to re-take any failures. Only one place was found where black and white could be developed, at the Casa Peña in Puerto Pollensa, and that took a week. Colour prints can be done in twenty-four hours, and Kodak transparencies can be sent to Madrid and should be returned in a week. The light can be very bright so it is easy to over expose especially if light is reflecting from the sea or white-walled houses. It is best to avoid midday photography whenever possible.

Police There are three different police forces in Spain and all are armed. The *Policia Municipal* wear blue uniforms and are attached to the local town halls and the *Policia Nacional* wear brown uniforms and berets or hats with a red stripe. The national police force is the *Guardia Civil*, whose uniform includes patent leather hats. The *Policia Nacional* is really an anti-crime squad, and it is the *Guardia Civil* who have the most power. All three services may be called upon if you need police help. The main police station is in Palma at Jose Antonia, 4. For the *Policia Nacional,* telephone 22 26 22 and for the *Policia Municipal,* telephone 28 16 00. There is a Lost Property office at the Town Hall, Plaza de Cort, telephone 22 77 44. If you want to stay and work on the island, you must apply to the police for a work permit.

Post offices The post offices, *correos,* are open from 09.00-14.00 hrs and from 16.00-19.00 hrs. Monday-Saturday. It is better to buy stamps *(sellos)* at a tobacconist *(estanco)* or from any shop selling post-cards or from a hotel reception desk. Mail boxes are yellow with a red stripe. A box labelled *extranjero* is for foreign-bound mail. Mail can be sent to a post office to be collected, if you do not know where you will be staying but have decided on a resort. The form of address is:

> Mr. & Mrs A.B.Smith
> Lista de Correos
> Puerto Pollensa
> Mallorca, Baleares
> Spain

Telephones are quite independent of post offices. (q.v.)

Railways See trains

Restaurants There is a wide choice of places to eat in every resort. Many bars also serve meals and most hotels offer meals to non-residents. Your own hotel will probably offer specialities at extra cost which you can order instead of the standard fare. Menus and prices are usually posted outside the entrance so that you can see what is available before choosing where to go, but a good plan is to ask your courier or other person with local knowledge to recommend somewhere. There is a wide range of prices but paying more may not mean a better meal, merely a more elaborate service. The menu will often be in more than one language including English, but in smaller places where you may get more authentic local cooking you will do best if you know some of the basic words for foods and dishes that may be on the menu. (See Food section, p.126 and language notes p.134.) The *menu del dia* is always very good value. This will be a two or three course meal with bread and wine, for 350-450pta, and may include a choice of starter and main course with fruit or ice cream. A meal for two with a bottle of wine in a more expensive restaurant may come to 3,000pta or more, depending what you have.

Shops and shopping See also markets. Shopping for food is easy everywhere on the island. Even the smallest villages have a general store or two and they are nearly all self service. Hours are 09.00-13.00 or 13.50 and 16.00 or 16.50-20.00, although most shops only open in the mornings on Saturdays. Pollensa and Alcudia markets are good places for fruit and vegetables and there is an excellent supermarket at Puerto Pollensa, the MIR shop recommended by Eddie Watkinson. If you want to go on a shopping trip to Palma it is best to get there early and finish before the long siesta time, or else use this opportunity to have a long leisurely meal at a restaurant offering Mallorquin specialities. Palma is a very big city. You will need a street plan to find your way round the maze of narrow streets in the old part. (There is one on the back of the Firestone map.) Another way of shopping is to visit the factories where goods are made and which have adjacent shops with supposedly discount prices. There are leather factories at Inca and simulated pearls at Manacor, and a glass-blowing factory between Inca and Pollensa.

Taxis These are cheaper than in Britain and can be good value for four people sharing. They are usually found queuing in main squares or in front of hotels, or you can ask a hotel receptionist to call one for you. The green sign *Libre* means free and any taxi displaying this can be flagged down. There is usually a board near the taxi rank displaying standard fares to nearby places. If you want to go on a long journey you will probably have to pay the fare both ways even if you are not returning. It is best to agree on the price before setting off. Tips of 5-10% of the fare are customary.

Telephones The telephone system has been modernised and most of the call boxes have automatic dialling facilities and can be used for international calls. They take 5-, 25- and 50- peseta coins, which are lined up in a slot on top of the dialling box which is a push-button type. Coins not used are refunded when you hang up. Most bars have telephones which can be used for local calls. The dialling tone is a single intermittent note and the engaged sign is a very rapid intermittent note. To make a call to England, first dial 07 for the international line, pause until you hear a continuous high-pitched tone, dial 44 for Great Britain, then the area code missing the first 0, (e.g. 61 for Manchester, not 061), then the number. A good supply of 50-peseta coins are needed, but it is cheaper after 8.00 p.m. and before 8.00 a.m., after 2.00 p.m. on Saturday and all day Sunday. If the coins refuse to go in the slot it means the box is full and you will have to find another telephone. If you are staying in a hotel, they will always make calls for you which you can take in your room, but there may be a surcharge. To make a personal call ask the operator for *persona a persona* and to reverse the charges ask for *cobro revertido*.

Theft In Palma and the busy resorts on the south coast it is necessary to be on guard against handbag-snatchers and pickpockets, as in most places in the world today. Such incidents are not common in the quieter areas in the north of the island, but not entirely unknown. Car thieves operate everywhere and it is never safe to leave valuables or indeed anything else in a car when you go off walking for the day. It is best to leave the car quite empty if possible, with the seats tipped forward to show there is nothing underneath. We learnt this the hard way, returning from a walk to find a shopping bag full of groceries had been taken, but considering ourselves lucky that other items such as waterproof clothing had been left.

Toilets There are very few public toilets in Mallorca. In bars, hotels etc there are usually pictorial signs for men and women. If you have to ask the phrase is *Dónde están los servicios?* (where are the toilets?)

Tourist offices The Spanish National Tourist Office at 57, St. James' St., London SW1A 1LD will supply lists of available accommodation and a brochure but do not undertake bookings. The offices in Mallorca are all in Palma, except that there is sometimes a small office attached to a town hall, as at Soller. The main office in Palma is at Avenida Jaime III, 10, tel. 21-22-16. There is also a Municipal tourist office at Calle Almudaina, tel. 22-40-82, and the Fomento del Turismo de Mallorca, A. Jose Antonio, 1, tel. 22-45-37 and 24-53-10. The opening hours are c.10.00-13.00 and 16.00-19.30.

Trains There are two railway lines on the island, Palma-Inca and Palma-Soller. The line to Artà was closed some years ago. It is the Soller line which is of interest to walkers of course as Soller is a good centre to stay in or to go for a day if you are staying in Palma. The two lines have two quite separate but adjacent stations in the Plaza España, that for Soller being separated from the bus station by the Inca line. The Soller line was built in 1912 and although electrified it still uses very attractive old carriages with brass ornaments. The train ride is itself a splendid experience, highly recommended. The 10.40 train is a special tourist one which stops for 10 minutes at a mirador high above the Soller valley. If you want to go on this get to the station in good time especially at peak holiday times as it is very popular. You may have to take standing room on the platforms between the carriages and if you get wedged between too many people you won't see the scenery. There is an equally old tram which runs from Soller town to the port, also quite exciting.

Train Times						
Palma	08.00	10.40	13.00	15.15	19.45	22.00*
Bunyola	08.26	11.08	13.26	15.40	20.10	22.25*
Soller	09.00	11.45	14.00	16.15	20.45	23.00*
* *						
Soller	06.45	09.15	11.50	14.10	18.20	21.00*
Bunyola	07.15	09.45	12.15	14.35	18.45	21.25*
Palma	07.45	10.15	12.50	15.10	19.20	22.00*

*Sundays and holidays only

Tramway
Departures from Soller
05.55 07.00 08.00 09.00 10.00 11.00 11.30 12.00 12.30 13.00 14.00 15.00 16.00 16.30 17.00 17.30 17.55 19.00 20.00 20.45
Departures from Puerto
06.20 07.30 08.25 09.30 10.30 11.30 12.00 13.00 13.25 14.30 15.30 16.30 17.00 17.30 17.55 18.30 19.30 20.20 21.10

TEUCRIUM SUBSPINOSIM

L'Ofre (Walk 25)

APPENDIX 2. LANGUAGE NOTES

Introduction Many people in Mallorca speak some English especially in the major tourist centres and in large hotels. Many others, particularly in the smaller villages and in the country do not know a single word of English or French or German or any other language, except Castilian Spanish and Mallorquin. These are the people you are most likely to meet when walking and it is well worth while taking the trouble to learn a few words and phrases so that you can pass the time of day with them.

The official language of Mallorca is Castilian Spanish, but this is a second language to many islanders who speak Mallorquin between themselves. Mallorquin is a dialect of Catalan and includes words of French and Arabic origin. With a knowledge of French and a little Spanish it is possible to get the gist of the written language, but the spoken language is another matter. On the other hand, because it is a second language, Castilian Spanish is spoken more slowly by the Mallorquins than by people from mainland Spain. This is a great help if you are just learning to speak Spanish.

The best way to learn is to listen to a cassette course such as the B.B.C. one listed on p.143, or to the B.B.C. combined radio and television course *Digame!* When you get to Mallorca, listen to Spanish people talking in shops and bars and so on and do not be shy about trying out what you have learned. Most people are very pleased that you try to speak their language and will be very helpful in speaking slowly and telling you how to say things.

Castilian is pronounced exactly as it is spelt, so that if you know the rules you can make a reasonable attempt at pronouncing any words you encounter. Stress is on the next to the last syllable unless indicated otherwise by a stress accent (é).

Key to pronunciation
The following guide is given for reference and to introduce a few words of vocabulary. It is no substitute for listening to people talking, on cassettes, radio or in real life.

a	between a in lass and in father	adiós	goodbye
b	as in English	banco	bank
c	before i and e like th in thin	cinco	five
	before anything else as in cat	cliente	customer
ch	as in church	chico	boy

d	at beginning of word, like d in dog	dos	two
	in other places, like th in though	verdad	true
e	as in men, but at end of word as in day	leche	milk
f	as in English	fácil	easy
g	before a, o, u, or consonant, as in gas	gasolina	petrol
	before e & i as ch in loch	gente	people
gu	before a, like gw	agua	water
h	always silent	hombre	man
i	between i in bit and in machine	litro	litre
j	like ch in loch	sopa de ajo	garlic soup
k	as in English (only used in foreign words)	kilo	kilo
l	as in English	libro	book
ll	like lli in million	me llamo	I'm called
m	as in English	mantequilla	butter
n	as in English	naranja	orange
ñ	as ni in onion	los niños	the children
o	between top and for	oficina	office
p	as in English	pan	bread
q	like English k	quizás	perhaps
r	slightly rolled	el norte	the north
rr	strongly rolled	carretera	main road
s	voiceless, as in sin	seis	six
t	as in English	tienda	shop
u	as in boot	usted	you
		ustedes	you (plural)
v	like a soft English b	un vaso de vino	a glass of wine
x	at end of word, like tch	Felanitx (placename)	
	between vowels, like gs	taxi	taxi
y	like y in yes	mayor	main
	(but the word y, meaning and, like i in machine)		
z	as th in thick	manzana	apple

N.B. The three double letters ch, ll, rr are considered as separate letters by the Spanish Academy so that they have separate sequences in Spanish dictionaries.

Brief glossary

Some very basic words and phrases are included here because it can be useful to have reference to them without carrying a separate book in your rucsac. Some useful phrasebooks are listed in the bibliography.

N.B. Question marks and exclamation marks are always used upside down at beginning of a question or exclamation.

Everyday words and expressions

hello	¡ ola!
good morning	buenos días
good afternoon	buenos tardes
goodnight	buenos noches
goodbye	adiós
see you later	hasta luego
yes/no	si/no
please	por favor
thank you	gracias
thats all right	de nada
thank you very much	muchas gracias
excuse me, sorry	perdóneme
I'm sorry	lo siento
I'm English	soy Inglés
I don't understand	no comprendo
would you repeat please?	¿ puede repetir por favor?
more slowly, please	más despacio, por favor
what did you say?	¿ como?
what is that?	¿ qúe es eso?
do you speak English?	¿ hable Ingles?
there is, there are	hay
is there a bank near here?	¿ hay un banco por aqui?
where is the post office?	¿ dónde está correos?
where are the toilets?	¿ dónde están los servicios?
men	señores/hombres/caballeros
women	señoras, mujeres
open/closed	abierto/cerrado
today/tomorrow/next week	hoy/mañana/la proxima semana
where can I buy...?	¿ dónde se puede comprar...?
a newspaper, stamps	un periódico, sellos

I'd like that	quiero eso...
I'll have this	tomo esto
how much is it?	i cuanto es?

Accommodation

do you hàve a room?	i tiene una habitación?
double, single	doble, individual
tonight	esta noche
for two/three nights	para dos/tres noches
how much is the room?	cuanto es la habitación?
with bath/without bath	con baño/sin baño

Bar and restaurant vocabulary

drinks	bebidas
breakfast	desayuno
lunch/dinner	comida/cena
I'd like/we'd like	quiero/queremos
I'll have/we'll have	tomo/tomamas
a black coffee	un café solo
two black coffees	dos cafés solos
a white coffee	un café con leche
three white coffees	tres cafés con leches
tea with milk	té con leche
tea with lemon for me	té con limon para mi
a beer	una cerveza
the house wine	el vino de la casa
a glass of red wine	un vaso de vino tinto
white wine	vino blanco
a dry sherry	un jerez seco
a bottle of mineral water	una botella de agua mineral
fizzy/still	con gas/sin gas
orange juice	zumo de naranja
soup	sopa
hors d'oeuvres	entremesas
eggs, egg dishes	huevos
fish, fish dishes	pescados
sea food, shell fish	mariscos
meat, meat dishes	carne
game	caza
vegetables	verduras/legumbres

137

cheese	queso
fruit	fruta
ice cream	helados
desserts	postres
sandwich	bocadillo
anything else?	¿ algo más?
nothing else thank you	nada más gracias
the bill, please	la cuenta, por favor
is service included?	¿ está incluido el servicio?
packed lunches	picnics
two packed lunches for tomorrow	dos picnics para mañana

Getting about

by car, on foot	en coche, a pie
how can I/we get to Soller?	¿ como se llega a Soller?
where is the bus station?	¿ dónde está la estacion de autobus?
the bus stop for Alcudia	la parada de autobus para Alcudia
how much is the fare	¿ cuanto vale el billete?
return	ida y volta
single	solamente ida
where is the road to Inca?	¿ dónde está la carretera a Inca?
where is the footpath to...?	¿ dónde está la senda a...?
where is the way to...?	¿ dónde está el camino a....?
may we go this way?	¿ se puede pasar por aqui?
is it far?	¿ está lejos?
how far?	¿ a qué distancia?
how long?	¿ cuanto tiempo?
very near?	muy cerca?
left/right	izquierda/derecha
straight on	todo recto
first left	la primera a la izquierda
second right	la segunda a la derecha
opposite the church	en frente de la iglesia
behind the hotel	detrés el hotel
at the end of the street	al final de la calle
after the bridge	después del puente
where are you going?	¿ adónde va/van ?
I'm going/we're going to...	voy a.../vamos a...
right of way	derecho de camino

138

Car travel

where can I/we rent a car?	¿ dónde se puede alquilar un coche?
how much is it per day?	¿ cuanto es por dia?
how much is it for a week?	¿ cuanto es por una semana?
petrol	gasolina
petrol station	estación de servicio
car repair shop	garaje/taller
standard petrol/premium petrol	normal/super
fill it up please	lleno, por favor
10, 20, 30 litres	diez, veinti, treinta litros
may I/we park here?	¿ se puede aparcar aqui?

Road signs

Most are international, but you may see these:

¡ Alto!	Halt!
Aparciamento	Parking
Calzada deteriorada	Bad road
Calzada estrecha	Narrow road
Ceda el paso	Give way
Cruce peligroso	Dangerous crossroads
Cuidada	Caution
Curva peligrosa	Dangerous bend
Despacio	Slow
Desviacion	Diversion
Desprediamentes	Falling stones
¡ Pare!	Stop !
Peligro	Danger
Prohibido adelantar	No overtaking
Prohibido aparco	No parking
Puesto de socorro	First aid post

Emergencies

Help! Fire!	¡ Socorro ¡ Fuego!
Police	Policia, Guardia Civil
I've had a breakdown	mi coche se ha estropeado
There's been an accident	ha habido un accidente
call a doctor quickly	llamen a un medico, rapidamente
it's urgent	es urgente

Placenames
Most places in Mallorca have two names, Castilian and Mallorquin, both of which are in common use. You will notice these variant spellings on maps, signposts and guidebooks, including this one. Although at first it is confusing, you very quickly become used to it and they are often very similar, e.g. La Calobra, Sa Calobra and La Puebla, Sa Pobla. You will also notice that whenever a road crosses a stream there is a signpost, and that usually the name has been altered in paint from Castilian to Mallorquin. Although Castilian is the official language on the island there are some who would like to see Mallorquin reinstated!

Some placename pronunciations

Cala San Vicente	Kah-lah San Bee-then-tay
Lluc	L'yook
Mallorca	My-orka
Pollensa	Pol-yen-sa
Soller	Sol-yer
Ternelles	Tern-ell-yes
Valdemossa	Vall-day-moh-sah

HIPPOCREPIS BALEARICA

APPENDIX 3. FURTHER READING

Walking guidebooks

Crespi-Green, Valerie. Landscapes of Mallorca: a countryside guide. London. Sunflower Books. 1984. 168p. illus.

The first book in English to describe any walks on the island. The descriptions are Palma-based and many depend on public transport. More useful for the general tourist than the experienced mountain walker, but a good and useful guide which includes car tours and picnic sites.

ICONA. Son Moragues: guia de paseo. Palma. 1982. 51p. illus.

This little booklet (in Spanish) gives a great deal of information about the Son Moragues Walk (No.26) including line-drawings of the flora and fauna. (Also published in Catalan)

Llofriu, Pere. Caminant per Mallorca. Barcelona. Publicacions de l'Abadia de Montserrat. 1983. 109p.

Describes 18 walks, of which only 5 coincide with the walks in the present book. Written in Catalan, and not very easy to use as the sketch maps are rather rudimentary. Includes notes on the flora and fauna pertaining to each walk.

Palos, Benigne. Itineraris de Muntanya: excursions a peu per la Serra de Mallorca. (Manuals d'introduccio a la naturalesa, 5) Palma. Editorial Moll. 2nd ed. 1984. 164p. illus.

Also in Catalan, but with very good sketch maps. Gives details of 40 mountain walks, most which are not covered in the present book. The descriptions can be followed to some extent if you have a knowledge of French and a smattering of other languages. The times given appear to be for experienced walkers who are also young and very fit. Recommended.

Ponce, Paco. Mallorca: ein Mallorquiner zeigt seine Heimat. Gerlen, 6601 Saarbrücken-Ensheim, West Germany, Repa-Druck. 2nd. enlarged ed. n.d. 128p. illus.

The author is a Mallorquin who lives in Soller and the German text was prepared by his wife, Dolly Ponce. Most of the 18 walks are in the Soller area and depend on public transport. Interspersed between the walk descriptions is information on plants and animals and the book ends with a section of Mallorquin recipes. Good photographs, some in colour. Recommended if you can read German.

Natural history books

General

Parrack, James D. The naturalist in Majorca. Newton Abbot: David and Charles. 1973. 224p. illus. o.p.

Unfortunately out-of-print but worth trying to obtain from libraries or searching for in secondhand bookshops. Includes a checklist of birds and a bibliography.

Birds

Bannerman, David A & Bannerman, W.Mary. The birds of the Balearics, illus. by Donald Watson. Croom Helm. 1983. 230p., 12 col. pl., 19 b. & w. pl., 34 line drawings.

A detailed and authoritative work with excellent illustrations. The colour plates reproduce paintings by Donald Watson and show c.50 species in their natural surroundings.

Heinzel, Hermann, Fitter, Richard & Parslow, John. The birds of Britain and Europe with North Africa and the Middle East. London. Collins. 1972. 320. illus.

Over 1,000 coloured illustrations and with distribution maps on the same page as the descriptions.

Peterson, Roger, Mountfort, Guy and Hollom, P.A.D. A field guide to the birds of Britain and Europe. 4th ed. London. Collins. 1983. 239p. illus.

Another excellent guide, but distribution maps separated from descriptions. Take both if you can as they complement each other.

Serra, Joan Mayol. Els aucells de les Balears. (Manuals d'introduccio a la naturelesa, 2) 2nd ed. Palma. Editorial Moll. 1981. 155p. illus.

A definitive work, but in Catalan. There is a useful checklist of birds arranged according to family and giving the names in Latin, local Balearic, Catalan, Castilian and English.

Watkinson, Eddie. A guide to bird-watching in Mallorca. 2nd ed. Alderney, J.G. Sanders. 1982. 64p. (From Natural History Book Service Ltd., Freepost, London SE21 8BR.)

Sometimes available from Casa Peña, Puerto de Pollensa or the newsagents on the Formentor road, 100m from the Pollensa road junction. Essential information on all the major sites as well as much general information.

Flowers

Bonner, Anthony, Plants of the Balearic islands. (Manuals d'introduccio a la naturelesa, 1) Palma. Editorial Moll. 1982. 150p. illus.

An excellent book with good line drawings, written for walkers, amateur botanists and nature lovers in general. Needs supplementing with one or more of the standard field guides, but indispensible to anyone interested in the flora met with on the walks. Available from the Casa Peña in Puerto de Pollensa. Good bibliography.

Polunin, Oleg and Huxley, Anthony. Flowers of the Mediterranean. Chatto and Windus. 1972. 260p. illus. (paperback).

A well illustrated guide, easy for the amateur to use.

Polunin, Oleg. Flowers of Europe; a field guide. Oxford U.P. 1969.

General interest

Berlitz travel guide: Majorca and Minorca. English ed. dist. by Cassell. 1982.

A useful pocket guidebook.

Facaros, Dana and Pauls, Michael. Mediterranean island hopping: the Spanish islands; a handbook for the independent traveller. London. Sphere Books. 1981. 264p.

A good general guidebook but may be difficult to obtain; I found a copy in a book sale. (The front cover is not the Formentor peninsula, but a reversed print of the Cavall Bernat ridge!)

Foss, Arthur. Majorca. Faber and Faber. 1972. 236p. o.p.

A historical survey with a good bibliography.

Graves, Robert & Hogarth, Paul. Majorca observed. London. Cassell. 1965. 150p. o.p.

Anecdotes about life on the island by the well-known writer who lived in Deyá from 1928 to his death in 1985 (except for the war years) and with illustrations by Hogarth.

Sand, George Winter in Majorca. Trans. and annotated by Robert Graves. Valldemosa. 1956. 200p.

George Sand spent the winter of 1838-9 on the island with Chopin at the *Cartuja* in Valldemosa. Interesting reading, but you need to get this edition which includes Quadrado's Refutation of George Sand written in 1841 and Robert Graves's notes to balance Sand's very biased account.

Thurston, Hazel. The travellers' guide to the Balearics: Majorca, Minorca, Ibiza and Formentera. London. Jonathan Cape. 1979. 366p.

A combination of practical information with history.

Language

BBC. Get by in Spanish: a quick beginners' course for holidaymakers and business people. 1977.

A booklet and two cassettes, available from bookshops or direct from the BBC at PO Box 234, London SE1 3TH.

D.L.Ellis, & R.Ellis. Travellers' Spanish. Pan Books. 1981.

A useful pocket phrasebook.

Ramon Sopena. n.d. Diccionario ITER. Catalán-Castellano y Castellano-Catálan. Barcelona.

In the absence of a Catalan-English dictionary this is quite a help in using any of the Catalan books listed, in conjunction with a Castilian-English dictionary of course.

Digame! A combined BBC television and radio course for beginners in Spanish BBC 1978.

Course book and three LP records or cassettes.

NOTES AND AMENDMENTS 1988

Walk 6. Atalaya de Albercuitx. The road from the Mirador d'es Colomer to the Atalaya has been upgraded from a rough track to a surfaced road. Best avoided at weekends.

Walk 12. Cuixat Gorge. Access difficult as the last house 'Las Corterados' has been found unoccupied and the gate locked. Follow a new road up through a housing development on the lower slopes of Cuarterada, then continue over the top of this hill. About 200m north of the top find a streambed descending ENE and follow this down into the gorge.

Walks 12, 14 and 15. Ternelles valley area. Access restrictions to this area are changing all the time. Please enquire locally before visiting this area.

Walk 17(a). Tomir by Aucanella. Finding the way out of the flat area near the abandoned house at Aucanella is not easy, because the fields have been overgrown with trees and large shrubs. When you arrive at the boundary fence here, turn left and follow the path to the house. It is then easier to follow the vestiges of the track which runs almost W for about 500m before turning N up to the Coll des Pedregaret.

Walk 18. Puig d'es Ca. The landowner of the Fartaritx property is still very hostile to walkers and has a gun.

Walk 20. Puig Roig. On the return route to Mossa there is a new track which leads from the oakwoods into the fields. I'm told it is easy to find and easier to follow than the old path.

Walk 22. Massanella. Near Comafreda the sign which used to read 'Puig de Massanella' etc. has gone. To follow the described route keep in the wood just outside the wall on the left of the field. Alternatively follow the new blue arrows which will also take you up to the Coll de Sa Linea track. Turn left when you reach it. The summit of Massanella has also changed since my last visit. The iron cross is no longer there but there is a new concrete trig point. To descend in mist the direction is SE.

Walks 26 and 27. Alaro and Alcadena. For K13, read K18.

GENERAL NOTES.

Maps. p.35. Maps may also be obtained from The Map Shop, 15, High Street, Upton-upon-Severn, Worcs., WR8 0HJ. The 1:50,000 Military Maps are supplied folded in a plastic wallet for £1.75 each plus postage. (1988 price list). When in stock they will be supplied by return post.

Buses. p.123. In winter 1988 the 09.30 bus from Puerto Soller to Deya etc. was running as on the summer timetable.

p.124. In winter the return bus from Puerto Pollensa to Soller leaves at 16.00 instead of 17.00.